A *beautiful* HEART

Heart-Healthy Recipes
for a Long, Happy Life

Elizabeth Epstein, MD

A beautiful HEART

Heart-Healthy Recipes for a Long, Happy Life

Copyright © 2019 Elizabeth Epstein, MD.

All rights reserved. No part of this book may be used or reproduced by any means, graphic, electronic, or mechanical, including photocopying, recording, taping or by any information storage retrieval system without the written permission of the author except in the case of brief quotations embodied in critical articles and reviews.

Balboa Press books may be ordered through booksellers or by contacting:

Balboa Press
A Division of Hay House
1663 Liberty Drive
Bloomington, IN 47403
www.balboapress.com
1 (877) 407-4847

Because of the dynamic nature of the Internet, any web addresses or links contained in this book may have changed since publication and may no longer be valid. The views expressed in this work are solely those of the author and do not necessarily reflect the views of the publisher, and the publisher hereby disclaims any responsibility for them.

Interior Image Credit:
Justin Galloway (food photographer)
Carolyn Pascual (food stylist)
Angela Agnew

ISBN: 978-1-9822-3416-4 (sc)
ISBN: 978-1-9822-3417-1 (e)
Print information available on the last page.

Balboa Press rev. date: 09/20/2019

Dear Gloria,

Wishing you every good thing and every blessing as you continue to take care of your Heart!

Warm Regards,
Samuel Youssef, MD

FOREWORD

Despite recent advances in diagnostic and treatment technologies, cardiovascular disease remains the leading cause of death for both men and women in the U.S. and worldwide. The link between diet and cardiovascular disease, especially the causative conditions of atherosclerosis and hypertension, has been clearly established on the basis of substantial scientific evidence across various study designs and research, including clinical trials. Dietary patterns that emphasize vegetables, fruits, and whole grains; include fish and shellfish, nuts, low-fat dairy products, and non-tropical vegetable oils; and limit intake of red and processed meat, sweets and sweetened beverages have the potential to prevent outcomes such as ischemic heart disease and stroke. However, patients are often overwhelmed by the perceived challenges of achieving a heart-healthy diet and view these recommendations as being restrictive and devoid of the pleasures of eating and sharing food and meals.

In her cookbook, Dr. Epstein presents a caring and loving approach that empowers and engages the reader to use creative and accessible foods, ingredients and recipes that emphasize the joy of food and ease of achieving a heart-healthy diet. Based on her experiences and recognition of the tendency to perceive cooking and eating healthy foods to require time, expense and skills in the kitchen, she compiled and tested recipes and strategies that are easy and achievable in addition to meeting the dietary guidelines to prevent cardiovascular disease. The cookbook provides creative recipes and helpful suggestions for achieving the recommended dietary pattern across several categories of foods: Breakfast, Appetizers and Snacks, Salads and Small Plates, Main Dishes and Entrees, and Desserts. The philosophy and empowering messages focus on nourishment as a goal that considers nutritional content but also fosters joyful interactions with food and cooking, as well as delicious meals.

Dr. Epstein's appreciation of the importance of having enjoyable experiences in the kitchen and the table is commendable. Her fresh and engaging approach should be well-received by patients, health care providers, and anyone aiming to achieve a heart-healthy diet without sacrificing the joy of cooking, eating and food.

Cheryl L. Rock, PhD, RD
Professor, Department of Family Medicine and Public Health
School of Medicine
University of California, San Diego

INTRODUCTION

A Beautiful Heart is a cookbook that belongs next to your favorite wooden spoon. If you don't yet have a favorite wooden spoon, if your kitchen is currently empty, overshadowed by alternative dining options that forego its use, this book will colonize the countertop and lead the way. Consider this as your new canvas for that accidental splatter of vibrant vegetable soup or incidental cloud of runaway cocoa powder. Consider this your invitation to paint your very own culinary Jackson Pollock! Because healthy eating and cooking can be messy—but it's a practice of art to work at every day.

This cookbook is about being creative, being brave, and learning how to translate healthy dietary principles into beautiful, delicious food that you can make with common, inexpensive ingredients. It's not about trendy ingredients or diet fads, not about flavonoids or polyphenols or medical mumbo-jumbo, not about what you can't eat and what you can, pitting the evil unhealthy vs. healthy. It's about the big picture: choosing an eating pattern that will promote long-term health—and rejoicing and taking pride in that choice. It's about nourishing your body with high quality, real food that you make at home. And its content and format are guided by the most recent scientific literature and the USDA and American Heart Association recommendations.

You don't have to be a chef, you don't have to be a nutritionist, and your food doesn't have to be perfect—that's why it's called a *practice*. All you have to do is decide if healthy eating is important to you, and if so, find the strength inside (strength you might not even know is there) to choose to try. Pay attention, focus, and as you proceed, notice what goes well and what could improve, be honest, listen to your body, appreciate your progress, and always try for better. Keep moving forward, from wherever you stand. Enjoy.

"Let food be thy medicine and medicine be thy food."

— Hippocrates

"So thoroughly and sincerely are we compelled to live, reverencing our life, and denying the possibility of change. This is the only way, we say; but there are as many ways as there can be drawn radii from one center."

— Henry David Thoreau

"Try new recipes, learn from your mistakes, be fearless, and above all have fun."

— Julia Child

We'll get started in 5…

5 *Let's get mindful.*

Why are you here, reading this cookbook? Maybe it's because your doctor recommended a new diet or maybe you decided you want to start working at a healthy eating pattern. Whatever your reason, set that intention. Write it below if you feel like it, or just keep it in your heart.

4 *Let's get scientific.*

Just kidding! There's no need to get into any complicated nutritional science here. You just need to keep a few simple principles in mind. We are aiming for a diet with lots of vegetables, fruit, legumes, whole grains, low-fat dairy, fish, and lean meats such as chicken or turkey. We are eliminating red meat, and we are minimizing salt and added sugar. And overall, we are minimizing empty calories and maximizing nutrition in each meal—even in decadent treats. There is robust evidence that this is the best diet for your heart. In fact, maintaining a healthy diet like this is one of the most important factors for ensuring long term heart health. That is why the American Heart Association made this diet part of its official recommendation for people of all ages.

› *Let's get quantitative.*

No matter how healthy your food is, there is still such a thing as too much. First and foremost, you must work to keep your portion size to the recommended amount. So check the serving size on each recipe and check yourself before you take seconds. Ask yourself if you really need it. Listen to your body.

2 *Let's get real.*

Making healthy lifestyle choices might not always be easy. And it isn't a perfect world. There may be times you feel you made the wrong choice, and that's okay. This is about a healthy eating pattern. Recognize areas where you can improve, and without judgment, move forward with the aim of working for better. As long as you are mindful, honest with yourself about what you want and need, and as long as you simply keep trying—then you are succeeding. Try to be kind to yourself, take pride your progress, and find joy in your healthy lifestyle. Because what's it all about anyway if we aren't enjoying life?

1 *Let's get cooking!*

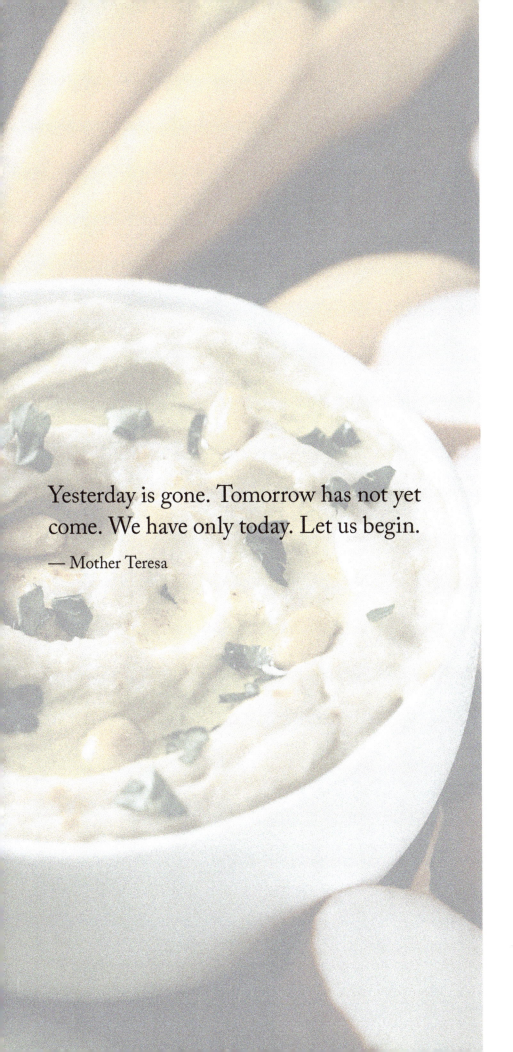

Yesterday is gone. Tomorrow has not yet come. We have only today. Let us begin.

— Mother Teresa

CONTENTS

Foreword

Introduction

Breakfast

    Corner Café Granola 3
    Daily Bread 4
    Avocado Toast with Creamy Scrambled Eggs 7
    Savory Tofu Scramble 8
    Super-Fluffy Protein Pancakes 11
    Hearty Oatmeal Pancakes 11
    Overnight Oats 12
    Make-Your-Own Almond Milk 15
    Creamy Stovetop Oats 16
    Tahini Dark Chocolate Chip Banana Bread 19
    Almond Butter Breakfast Bread 20

Appetizers & Snacks

    From-the-fields Oat Crackers 25
    Hummus-in-a-hurry 25
    Creamy Avocado Pesto 26
    Classic Basil Pesto 26
    Nacho Everyday Nachos 29
    Peachy Green Smoothie 30
    Daily Dose Wellness Smoothie 30
    Crispy Cauliflower Bites 33
    Mini Potato Wedges 34
    Peanut Fudge-Crunch Snack Bars 37
    Blueberry Cashew Shortbread Bars 38

Sandwiches & Small Plates

    Almond Butter Sweet Potato Toast 43
    Sweet Potato Falafels 44
    Not-So-Secret Sauce Sandwich 47
    Open Face Curried & Classic Chickpea Salad Sandwich 48
    Make-Your-Own Mayo 51
    Crispy Salmon Cakes 52
    Mediterranean Stuffed Peppers 55
    Balance Bowls 56
    Veggie Spice Quesadillas 59

SALADS & SIDE DISHES

Refreshing Arugula Salad 63
Mediterranean Masterpiece Salad 64
Crispy Seared Tofu 67
White Bean & Kale Salad 68
Roasted Veggie Salad with Creamy Avocado Dressing 71
Hearty Roasted Kabocha Squash 72
Kale Caesar Salad with Blackened Tempeh 75
Tender Sautéed Greens 76
Spiced Cauliflower Rice 79
Curried Cauliflower Quinoa 80

MAIN DISHES & ENTREES

California Quinoa Bowl with Not-so-secret Sauce 85
Moroccan Broccoli & Tofu Quinoa Bowl 86
Twice-Baked Santa Fe Sweet Potatoes with Cilantro Crema 89
Cilantro Crema 90
San Diego Black Bean Burger Stacks 93
Chinese Fried Rice 94
Miso Pesto Soba Noodles 97
Easy Split Peasy Soup 98
Indian Lentil Daal with Bell Peppers 98
Saag Tofu "Paneer" 101
Oven-Roasted Salmon 102
Keen Green Quinoa Casserole 105
Quinoa Lasagna 106
Alfredo Pasta with Broccoli & Spinach 109
Pesto Pasta with Oven-Roasted Tomatoes 110

DESSERTS

Tahini Cookies 115
Oatmeal Chocolate Chip Cookies 116
Chocolate Cake with Butterless Chocolate Buttercream 119
Chunky Chocolate-Almond Frozen Yogurt 120
Strawberry Frozen Yogurt 123
Cinnamon Roll Blondies 124
Berry Delicious Cake 127
Gooey Black Bean Brownies 128
Tahini Brownies 128
Raw Walnut Fudge Brownies 131

BREAKFAST

CORNER CAFÉ GRANOLA
Serves 9

The combination of homemade granola and Greek yogurt or a thick smoothie juxtaposes whole-grain-crunch with a cool creaminess that creates the perfect bite—and the perfect companion for a delicious serving of fresh fruit.

---

1 cup slivered almonds, toasted
2 ½ cups old fashioned oats
1 cup shredded coconut
¼ cup dark honey or maple syrup
¼ cup vegetable oil
¼ tsp salt

Preheat oven to 350°F. As the oven is preheating, pop the almonds into the oven on a baking sheet.

Meanwhile, mix together the remaining ingredients in a medium-sized bowl. Once the almonds are a bit toasty, about 10 minutes, add the almonds and do one final mix.

Spread the granola mixture onto a large baking sheet. Bake for 30 minutes, stirring every 10 minutes or so if you think of it—this helps the granola brown evenly and prevents burning. Serve atop yogurt or a smoothie.

Serving size (62g = ½ cup)
Amount per serving: Calories 300% Daily Value, Total Fat 18g - 23%, Saturated Fat 4.5g - 23%, Trans Fat 0g, Cholesterol 0mg - 0%, Sodium 85mg - 4%, Total Carbohydrate 31g - 11%, Dietary Fiber 4g - 4%, Total Sugars 14g, Added Sugars 8g - 16%, Protein 6g, Vitamin D 0mcg - 0%, Calcium 47mg - 4%, Iron 2mg - 10%, Potassium 219mg - 4%

DAILY BREAD
Serves 14

Ballymaloe House and Cookery School in Cork, Ireland, is a culinary wonderland, where fresh, real, good food made with ingredients from their 100-acre organic farm and greenhouse is an everyday reality. Early in the morning, the head pastry chef bakes loaves upon loaves of fresh bread whose heavenly scent imbibes the premises with the joy of a new day. This recipe is their classic brown bread for everyday—morning, noon, or night. It is incredibly simple, full of whole grains, and a microcosm of the Ballymaloe experience: fresh out of the oven, it is something sacred, made by hand with the utmost care. Although using yeast might sound intimidating, this recipe is easy as can be, requires no kneading, and always results in a delicious loaf without demanding perfection.

---

3 ½ cups whole wheat flour
½ cup white flour (all-purpose or bread flour)
1 tsp salt
Generous ½ cup plus 1 ½ cups tepid water - 2 cups total
1 tbsp dark molasses
2 ½ tsp active dry yeast

Mix flours and salt in a large bowl.

Measure out ½ cup water and stir in molasses and yeast. Let mixture stand for 10 minutes.

Add remaining 1 ½ cups water to yeast mixture. Combine wet and dry and let batter stand for 10 minutes.

Line 9-in loaf pan with parchment paper and pour in the dough. Drape a towel over the pan and allow to rise in a cozy place for 20 minutes. Preheat oven to 450°F.

Bake for 20 minutes. Decrease oven temp to 400°F, take out of the oven, and remove loaf from the pan.

Pop the loaf back in the oven upside down directly on the rack and bake another 15 minutes.

Serving size (71g = 1 slice)
Amount per serving: Calories 120 - % Daily Value, Total Fat 1g - 1%, Saturated Fat 0g - 0%, Trans Fat 0g, Cholesterol 0mg - 0%, Sodium 140mg - 6%, Total Carbohydrate 26g - 9%, Dietary Fiber 4g - 14%, Total Sugars 1g, Added Sugars 1g - 2%, Protein 5g, Vitamin D 0mcg - 0%, Calcium 5mg - 2%, Iron 1mg - 6%, Potassium 141mg - 4%,

AVOCADO TOAST WITH CREAMY SCRAMBLED EGGS
Serves 2

Scrambled eggs are a timeless breakfast classic for a reason. However simple they are, they never cease to satisfy and nourish. The secret to the dreamy creaminess in this recipe is low heat and constant stirring.

---

1 medium avocado
4 eggs
2 tbsp milk

Optional
1 tsp Dijon mustard
½ tsp minced fresh thyme or ¼ tsp dried leaf thyme
1 tbsp butter
About ½ cup cheddar cheese, grated
1 tbsp chives
Pinch of freshly ground black pepper
Salt to taste

Cut two pieces of Daily Bread, toast, and set aside.

Scoop insides of avocado into a small bowl and mash well with a fork. Spread avocado mash onto toast. Meanwhile, whisk eggs with milk, mustard, and thyme if desired.

Spray a medium skillet with nonstick spray, heat, and pour in the eggs. Cook over very low heat, stirring frequently, until the eggs have formed into a creamy mass, about 5-8 minutes.

Pop eggs on top of avocado. Sprinkle with chives, salt and pepper.

Serving size (266g)
Amount per serving: Calories 400, % Daily Value, Total Fat 20g - 26%, Saturated Fat 3.5g - 18%, Trans Fat 0g, Cholesterol 350mg - 117%, Sodium 300mg - 13%, Total Carbohydrate 35g - 13%, Dietary Fiber 6g - 21%, Total Sugars 2g, AddedSugars 1g - 2%, Protein 20g, Vitamin D 4mcg - 20%, Calcium 37mg - 2%, Iron 2mg - 10%, Potassium 496mg - 10%

SAVORY TOFU SCRAMBLE
Serves 3

Tofu is a powerful source of protein and micronutrients with its own shockingly substantial slew of health benefits. Plus, it's versatile and delicious. Many avoid using it, wrongly assuming it lacks flavor, but it's just a matter of preparing it with a little pizzazz!

½ onion, diced
½ green bell pepper, diced
1 block tofu, drained and pressed
2 tbsp olive oil
1 tsp garlic powder
1 tsp onion powder
1 tbsp low-sodium soy sauce
½ tsp turmeric
2 tbsp nutritional yeast

Place tofu on a cutting board with a couple layers of paper towel on top. Put a plate on top of the paper towels and press to squeeze water out of the tofu.

Crumble tofu into a medium bowl. Add spices, nutritional yeast, and soy sauce, and mix. Set aside.

Heat a large skillet or frying pan (nonstick or sprayed with nonstick spray) and sauté the chopped onion and pepper for 3-5 minutes over medium heat, stirring frequently until onion begins to brown.

Add the tofu mixture. Cook for 5-7 more minutes, stirring frequently. Serve with a slice of daily bread or maybe even some tender sautéed greens!

Serving size (169g)
Amount per serving: Calories 150, % Daily Value, Total Fat 7g - 9%, Saturated Fat 0.5g - 3%, Trans Fat 0g, Cholesterol 0mg - 0%, Sodium 210mg - 9%, Total Carbohydrate 7g - 3%, Dietary Fiber 2g - 7%, Total Sugars 2g, Added Sugars 0g - 0%, Protein 16g, Vitamin D 0mcg - 0%, Calcium 212mg - 15%, Iron 3mg - 15%, Potassium 146mg - 4%

SUPER-FLUFFY PROTEIN PANCAKES
Serves 4

A gorgeous plate of fluffy pancakes is the hallmark of a relaxing, life-giving weekend. It seems that the fluffier the pancake, the more it dazzles and delights. These pancakes are of the fluffiest kind, but their nutritional strength lies in their higher protein content, which will fill the belly and fuel the day.

---

1 ½ cups Greek yogurt
⅔ cup whole wheat flour
⅓ cup all-purpose flour
2 eggs
2 tsp baking soda
½ tsp salt

In a medium-sized bowl, whisk together Greek yogurt and eggs.

Add flour and baking soda and mix thoroughly. You will have yourself a thick batter.

Heat a nonstick skillet (or frying pan sprayed with nonstick spray) over low heat. On my stove, they cook best at a 2.

Scoop ~1/3 cup batter onto pan and spread it out a bit. Slowly cook each side until golden brown, about 3 minutes each side.

Serve with butter, maple syrup, or maybe some fresh berries!

Serving size (164g = ~2 large pancakes)
Amount per serving: Calories 200, % Daily Value, Total Fat 2.5g - 3%, Saturated Fat 1g - 5%, Trans Fat 0g, Cholesterol 110mg - 37%, Sodium 950mg - 41%, Total Carbohydrate 28g - 10%, Dietary Fiber 2g - 7%, Total Sugars 3g, Added Sugars 0g - 0%, Protein 17g, Vitamin D 0mcg - 0%, Calcium 123mg - 10%, Iron 2mg - 10%, Potassium 256mg - 6%

HEARTY OATMEAL PANCAKES
Serves 4

Good old-fashioned diner breakfasts never disappoint, and oatmeal pancakes are always a tantalizing menu option. Channeling the time-honored diner experience but dropping the greasy spoon and adding whole grains, more fiber, and protein, these pancakes are an oft-requested family favorite.

---

1 1/3 cups milk (cow's, cashew, or almond milk)
1 tbsp cider vinegar
1 ½ tbsp vegetable oil
2 tsp vanilla
1 egg
2 cups rolled oats
2 tsp baking powder
½ tsp baking soda
¼ tsp salt

Mix cider vinegar and milk of choice together and set aside for a moment.

Place all ingredients in a blender or food processor, adding the cider-milk mixture last, and blend, blend, blend! If you'd like to leave some oatmeal texture, don't puree completely.

Heat nonstick or sprayed skillet over low-medium heat and drop about ¼ cup batter onto pan. Heat until bubbles appear on the surface of the pancakes, then flip, and cook for about a minute or 2 longer. Repeat with remainder of batter, and enjoy!

Serving size (135g = 2-3 pancakes)
Amount per serving: Calories 190, % Daily Value, Total Fat 5g - 6%, Saturated Fat 1g - 5%, Trans Fat 0g, Cholesterol 45mg - 15%, Sodium 350mg - 15%, Total Carbohydrate 29g - 11%, Dietary Fiber 4g - 14%, Total Sugars 1g, Added Sugars 0g - 0%, Protein 7g, Vitamin D 1mcg - 6%, Calcium 387mg - 30%, Iron 2mg - 10%, Potassium 219mg - 4%

OVERNIGHT OATS
Serves 1

Overnight oats are a cool, creamy version of the classic bowl of piping hot oatmeal and a great way to prepare breakfast ahead of time. Just before bed, throw these ingredients together in a jar and pop it in the fridge. In the morning, take that blank canvas and add whatever toppings are on hand. Create something beautiful!

½ cup oats
½ cup almond, soy, or 1% milk
½ tsp vanilla
Optional: 1 tbsp pumpkin seeds, 1 tbsp chia seeds, ½ tsp agave, 1 tbsp raisins/dried cranberries
Suggested toppings: walnuts, fresh blueberries, banana, almond butter, coconut, maple syrup, more almond milk

Combine all ingredients in Tupperware or jar and stir well. Refrigerate a couple hours or overnight. In the morning, stir, add those toppings, and make it a work of art!

Serving size (156g)
Amount per serving: Calories 180, % Daily Value, Total Fat 4.5g - 6%, Saturated Fat 0.5g - 3%, Trans Fat 0g, Cholesterol 0mg - 0%, Sodium 90mg - 4%, Total Carbohydrate 28g - 10%, Dietary Fiber 4g - 14%, Total Sugars 1g, Added Sugars 0g - 0%, Protein 6g, Vitamin D 1mcg - 6%, Calcium 120mg - 10%, Iron 2mg - 10%, Potassium 248mg - 6%

MAKE-YOUR-OWN ALMOND MILK

The taste of this creamy almond beverage is really something special. Add it to overnight oats, coffee, or even enjoy a nice cold glass it by itself.

1 cup almonds
½ tsp cinnamon
¼ tsp salt
1 tsp vanilla
4 cups water

Put all ingredients in blender and blend on high. Strain with a cheese cloth or nut bag and store in jars for the week ahead!

CREAMY STOVETOP OATS
Serves 1

This classic recipe for stick-to-your-ribs oats couldn't be simpler, but sometimes simple is best. Use this technique for the creamiest bowl of oatmeal imaginable.

½ cup rolled oats (per person)
1 cup water (per person)
¼ tsp salt (per person)
Recommended toppings: apple, mixed berries, cinnamon, brown sugar, banana, walnuts, butter, maple syrup, or any creative combination thereof

---

In a saucepan, add all ingredients. Cover and bring to a vigorous, rolling boil. Give the oats a good stir and turn off the stove. Let it sit on the burner for a few minutes while you're prepping your amazing toppings, and then you're ready for a heart-warming breakfast!

Serving size (278g)
Amount per serving: Calories 150, % Daily Value, Total Fat 3g - 4%, Saturated Fat 0.5g - 3%, Trans Fat 0g, Cholesterol 0mg - 0%, Sodium 490mg - 21%, Total Carbohydrate 27g - 10%, Dietary Fiber 4g - 14%, Total Sugars 1g, Added Sugars 0g - 0%, Protein 5g, Vitamin D 0mcg - 0%, Calcium 27mg - 2%, Iron 1mg - 6%, Potassium 150mg - 4%

TAHINI DARK CHOCOLATE CHIP BANANA BREAD
Serves 16

Waking up early enough to sit down, drink coffee, eat breakfast, and do a bit of reading is a daily practice that honors the morning, with gratitude for its consistent promise of a new day. However, time has a way of eluding even the most committed morning-lovers sometimes. This heavenly banana bread still does the morning proud but can be enjoyed on the go.

---

2 large ripe bananas
1/3 cup tahini
¼ cup maple syrup
2 eggs
1 tsp vanilla
1 ¾ cups almond flour
1 tsp baking soda
¼ tsp salt
½ cup dark chocolate chips

Preheat oven to 350°F.

Mash bananas in a large mixing bowl. Add tahini, maple syrup, and eggs and mix thoroughly. Stir in the remaining ingredients.

Pour into a loaf pan lined with parchment paper and sprinkle with toasted sesame seeds and dark chocolate chips if desired. Bake for 45-50 minutes.

Serving size (49g = 1 slice)
Amount per serving: Calories 170, % Daily Value, Total Fat 11g - 14%, Saturated Fat 2g - 110%, Trans Fat 0g, Cholesterol 20mg - 17%, Sodium 125mg - 5%, Total Carbohydrate 13g - 15%, Dietary Fiber 2g - 17%, Total Sugars 8g, Added Sugars 3g - 16%, Protein 5g, Vitamin D 0mcg - 10%, Calcium 39mg - 14%, Iron 1mg - 16%, Potassium 87mg - 12%

ALMOND BUTTER BREAKFAST BREAD
Serves 9

Here is another grab-and-go breakfast option or the perfect baked appetizer to start off a healthy brunch. This bread is so easy to throw together, and like magic, it becomes a delicious morning treat.

½ cup almond butter
2 eggs
2 tbsp dark honey
1 tsp vanilla
¼ tsp salt
¼ tsp baking soda
1 tbsp cinnamon

Preheat oven to 325°F. Mix all ingredients in a medium bowl. Pour into an 8x8 pan lined with parchment paper. Bake for 12-15 minutes.

Serving size (32g)
Amount per serving: Calories 120, % Daily Value, Total Fat 9g - 12%, Saturated Fat 1g - 5%, Trans Fat 0g, Cholesterol 40mg - 13%, Sodium 135mg - 6%, Total Carbohydrate 7g - 3%, Dietary Fiber 2g - 7%, Total Sugars 5g, Added Sugars 4g - 8%, Protein 4g, Vitamin D 0mcg - 0%, Calcium 58mg - 4%, Iron 1mg - 6%, Potassium 113mg - 2%

APPETIZERS & SNACKS

FROM-THE-FIELDS OAT CRACKERS
Serves 10

These simple, versatile crackers boast a down-to-earth taste of nature, whole grains, and pure ingredients and act as the perfect vessel for all manner of dips and spreads. Serve them with hummus or pesto for a tasty appetizer that begs to be enjoyed over good conversation with loved ones.

---

1 ½ cups old-fashioned oats
1 cup whole wheat flour
½ tsp salt
1 tbsp white sugar
½ cup water
5 tbsp olive oil

Preheat oven to 350°F. Blend oats to flour in a high-power blender or food processor.

In a large bowl, whisk together oat flour, wheat flour, salt, and sugar.

Pour in water and olive oil and mix until it comes together into a dough. Add a little more water if needed.

Roll the dough as thin as possible on a parchment paper lined baking sheet. Using a knife, score the dough by partially slicing through it to outline small squares.

Bake until lightly browned, about 15 minutes. Allow to cool completely.

Once cooled, it will be nice & crisp. Break along the lines into individual crackers and serve with hummus, pesto, or not-so-secret sauce.

Serving size (32g = ~5 crackers)
Amount per serving: Calories 150, % Daily Value, Total Fat 8g - 10%, Saturated Fat 1g - 5%, Trans Fat 0g, Cholesterol 0mg - 0%, Sodium 95mg - 4%, Total Carbohydrate 18g - 7%, Dietary Fiber 2g - 7%, Total Sugars 2g, Added Sugars 1g - 2%, Protein 3g, Vitamin D 0mcg - 0%, Calcium 10mg - 0%, Iron 1mg - 6%, Potassium 89mg - 2%

HUMMUS-IN-A-HURRY
Serves 10

Hummus is a creamy dollop of goodness that can be enjoyed as an appetizer, on top of salads, or in sandwiches or wraps. This recipe is easy as can be, low cost, and adaptable. And thank goodness—because one never knows when one might need hummus in a hurry!

---

1 15-oz can chickpeas or white beans, drained and rinsed
1 clove garlic
1/8- ¼ cup olive oil
2 tbsp lemon juice
2 tbsp tahini (can sub toasted sesame seeds or omit entirely)
1 tsp ground cumin
¼ tsp paprika (can used smoked paprika for a smoky flavor)

Add all ingredients to a blender or food processor and blend until creamy.

Measure out ¼ cup olive oil. While blending on low, pour in just enough oil to reach your desired consistency.

Enjoy with From-the-Field Oat Cracker on salads, or on a sandwich!

Serving size (54g)
Amount per serving: Calories 80, % Daily Value, Total Fat 5g - 6%, Saturated Fat 0.5g - 3%, Trans Fat 0g, Cholesterol 0mg - 0%, Sodium 125mg - 5%, Total Carbohydrate 7g - 3%, Dietary Fiber 2g - 7%, Total Sugars 0g, Added Sugars 0g - 0%, Protein 3g, Vitamin D 0mcg - 0%, Calcium 24mg - 2%, Iron 1mg - 6%, Potassium 89mg - 2%

Pesto is a welcomed addition to pasta, pizza, crackers, or even a sandwich, contributing not only flavor, but also greens and healthy fats. These two recipes each have their own unique nutrients and creamy factor—avocado in one and tofu in the other.

CREAMY AVOCADO PESTO
Serves 6

½ cup pistachios
¼ cup hemp hearts
2 cloves garlic
¼ tsp salt
2 medium avocados
½ cup olive oil

Add all ingredients except olive oil to a high-power blender or food processor and blend until smooth.

While blending on low, slowly drizzle in just enough olive oil and water to give your desired texture. Add extra water if the mixture is too thick.

Serve with wheat crackers or use on pasta!

Serving size (72g)
Amount per serving: Calories 230% Daily ValueTotal Fat 22g - 28%, Saturated Fat 2.5g - 13%, Trans Fat 0g, Cholesterol 0mg - 0%, Sodium 110mg - 5%, Total Carbohydrate 7g - 3%, Dietary Fiber 2g - 7%, Total Sugars 0g, Added Sugars 0g - 0%, Protein 5g, Vitamin D 0mcg - 0%, Calcium 10mg - 0%, Iron 1mg - 6%, Potassium 364mg - 8%

CLASSIC BASIL PESTO
Serves 6

2 cups basil or arugula, packed
¼ cup pine nuts, toasted
4 cloves garlic, peeled and chopped
2 tsp lemon juice
¼ tsp salt
½ package extra-firm silken tofu
(about 6 ounces), drained
¼ cup nutritional yeast (optional)

Add all ingredients to a blender and blend until creamy.

Serve with wheat crackers or use on pasta!

Serving size (49g)
Amount per serving: Calories 60, % Daily Value, Total Fat 4g - 5%, Saturated Fat 0g - 0%, Trans Fat 0g, Cholesterol 0mg - 0%, Sodium 25mg - 1%, Total Carbohydrate 3g - 1%, Dietary Fiber 1g - 4%, Total Sugars 1g, Added Sugars 0g - 0%, Protein 4g, Vitamin D 0mcg - 0%, Calcium 31mg - 2%, Iron 1mg - 6%, Potassium 110mg - 2%

NACHO EVERYDAY NACHOS
Serves 6

These nachos are irrefutable evidence that healthy food and delicious, indulgent food are not mutually exclusive. With secret nutrition hidden in the queso sauce, this recipe transforms the traditional not-so-healthy cheese into a nourishing dose of vegetables and protein, all while preserving the cheesy magic of a legendary plate of nachos.

For queso:
- 1 cup silken tofu
- ½ cup cooked carrots (can use canned)
- 1-2 tbsp chopped fresh seeded jalapeño
- 1 tbsp lemon juice
- 1 tsp apple cider vinegar
- 1 tsp garlic powder
- 1 tsp onion powder
- 1 tbsp nutritional yeast (optional)
- ½ tsp smoked paprika
- ½ tsp salt

For nachos:
- 6 100% whole wheat or corn tortillas
- 1 tomato, chopped small
- ½ medium avocado, chopped
- 1 15-oz can black beans, warmed on the stove

To make the chips, preheat oven to 350°F. Cut tortillas into small triangles, place on a baking sheet, and bake 5 minutes. Flip chips over, bake another 5 minutes, and you're done!

To make the queso, blend all ingredients in a blender. Done!

To assemble nachos, place chips on the bottom. Add black beans, then tomato and avocado. Warm queso on the stove for a couple minutes, then drizzle all over the top. Serve 'em up!

Serving size (194g)
Amount per serving: Calories 160, % Daily Value, Total Fat 4g - 5%, Saturated Fat 0g - 0%, Trans Fat 0g, Cholesterol 0mg - 0%, Sodium 270mg - 12%, Total Carbohydrate 25g - 9%, Dietary Fiber 6g - 21%, Total Sugars 3g, Added Sugars 0g - 0%, Protein 8g, Vitamin D 0mcg - 0%, Calcium 70mg - 6%, Iron 2mg - 10%, Potassium 482mg - 10%

Smoothies are a clever way to combine all manner of healthy ingredients into one cool, refreshing beverage that tastes like a deliciously indulgent milkshake.

PEACHY GREEN SMOOTHIE
Serves 1

---

1 packed cup spinach or kale
1 cup frozen mango
½ cup frozen peaches
½-inch piece of ginger, skin removed
1 cup 1% milk, soy milk, or almond milk

Blend all ingredients in a blender until creamy.

Serving size (529g)
servings per container
Amount per serving: Calories 210, % Daily Value, Total Fat 3g - 4%, Saturated Fat 0g - 0%, Trans Fat 0g, Cholesterol 0mg - 0%, Sodium 190mg - 8%, Total Carbohydrate 45g - 16%, Dietary Fiber 4g - 14%, Total Sugars 35g, Added Sugars 0g - 0%, Protein 2g, Vitamin D 2mcg - 10%, Calcium 252mg - 20%, Iron 1mg - 6%, Potassium 293mg - 6%

DAILY DOSE WELLNESS SMOOTHIE
Serves 1

---

1 medium banana, peeled then frozen
½ cup frozen berries
1 tbsp flaxseed meal (optional)
tbsp (1 ½ tsp) peanut butter
½ - ¾ cup 1% milk, soy milk, or almond milk
2 cups spinach or kale

Note: if you want to make a thick smoothie to eat with a spoon and maybe a little granola, use only 1/2 cup milk. For a drinkable smoothie, add 3/4 cup milk.

Serving size (361g)
Amount per serving: Calories 250, % Daily Value, Total Fat 7g - 9%, Saturated Fat 1g - 5%, Trans Fat 0g, Cholesterol 0mg - 0%, Sodium 125mg - 5%, Total Carbohydrate 44g - 16%, Dietary Fiber 9g - 32%, Total Sugars 23g, Added Sugars 0g - 0%, Protein 6g, Vitamin D 1mcg - 6%, Calcium 168mg - 15%, Iron 3mg - 15%, Potassium 668mg - 15%

CRISPY CAULIFLOWER BITES
Serves 4

Cauliflower is an astoundingly versatile hero-of-a-vegetable. Here it stars as an addicting appetizer that is oh-so-satisfying with a good dip.

---

1 head cauliflower (~12 oz) or 12-oz bag of cauliflower florets
2 tbsp olive oil
¼ tsp turmeric
¼ tsp garlic powder
¼ tsp onion powder
½ tsp salt

Preheat oven to 400°F.

Break cauliflower into florets and place directly on a baking sheet lined with parchment paper or aluminum foil.

Drizzle olive oil over cauliflower. Then sprinkle on turmeric, garlic powder, onion powder, and salt. Toss with your hands so that florets are evenly coated with olive oil and spices.

Bake for 55 minutes (or until nice n crispy), turning the pieces over halfway through. Serve with Not-So-Secret Sauce for dipping!

Serving size (93g)
Amount per serving: Calories 80, % Daily Value, Total Fat 7g - 9%, Saturated Fat 1g - 5%, Trans Fat 0g, Cholesterol 0mg - 0%, Sodium 270mg - 12%, Total Carbohydrate 5g - 2%, Dietary Fiber 2g - 7%, Total Sugars 2g, Added Sugars 0g - 0%, Protein 2g, Vitamin D 0mcg - 0%, Calcium 20mg - 2%, Iron 0mg - 0%, Potassium 261mg - 6%

MINI POTATO WEDGES
Serves 8

Potatoes get a bad reputation in terms of health because of their misplacement in the fryer. However, potatoes are actually a root vegetable that packs vitamins and nutrients. This recipe gives the infamous experience of fries without diminishing the nutritional value of the down-to-earth vegetable itself.

---

3 lbs red potatoes (or multi-color tiny potatoes), cut into small wedges
2 tsp garlic powder
2 tbsp nutritional yeast
Salt and pepper

Preheat oven to 425°F. Add potato wedges to a large baking sheet lined with aluminum foil (or use two baking sheets). Add the remaining ingredients and toss thoroughly.

Bake for 20 minutes, toss, then bake another 20 minutes. Pair these with Not-So-Secret Sauce or Cilantro Crema, and you'll never eat a French fry again!

Serving size (175g)
Amount per serving: Calories 190, % Daily Value, Total Fat 3.5g - 4%, Saturated Fat 0.5g - 3%, Trans Fat 0g, Cholesterol 0mg - 0%, Sodium 140mg - 6%, Total Carbohydrate 34g - 12%, Dietary Fiber 3g - 11%, Total Sugars 2g, Added Sugars 0g - 0%, Protein 5g, Vitamin D 0mcg - 0%, Calcium 16mg - 2%, Iron 1mg - 6%, Potassium 953mg - 20%

PEANUT FUDGE-CRUNCH SNACK BARS
Serves 8

Snacks are often the unsung heroes of the day, keeping the body satisfied during long stretches between meals. They facilitate mindfulness and presence in the here-and-now by undermining thoughts about meals yet to come brought about by a grumbling tummy. This recipe is a favorite snack bar to whip up every few weeks and pop in the refrigerator or freezer.

---

1 cup peanut butter
3 tbsp dark honey
½ tsp vanilla
¼ cup shredded coconut
½ cup old-fashioned rolled oats
¼ cup flaxseed meal
¼ cup dark chocolate chips (optional)

Line a loaf pan with parchment paper.

If peanut butter is hard, soften on the stove or in the microwave. I usually heat about an inch of water in a small pot and place my bowl on top of it to heat slightly. Mix together peanut butter, agave, and vanilla until smooth.

Pulse the oats and flaxseed meal together in a blender or food processor.

Add to the peanut butter mixture along with coconut and chocolate chips. Mix thoroughly. The mixture will become very thick and dry and you may even have some dry crumblies that you can't mix into the main mass—that's ok!

Dump everything into the loaf pan and press, press, press! Press it in really tight—that's how it's going to stay together! Now pop in the freezer for half an hour to help solidify. Remove from freezer and cut into 8 bars. Place them back in the freezer or refrigerator to store until you're ready to enjoy them.

Serving size (37g = 1 bar)
Amount per serving: Calories 200, % Daily Value, Total Fat 15g - 19%, Saturated Fat 5g - 25%, Trans Fat 0g, Cholesterol 0mg - 0%, Sodium 5mg 0%, Total Carbohydrate 14g - 5%, Dietary Fiber 2g - 7%, Total Sugars 7g, Added Sugars 4g - 8%, Protein 5g, Vitamin D 0mcg - 0%, Calcium 22mg - 2%, Iron 1mg - 6%, Potassium 144mg - 4%

BLUEBERRY CASHEW SHORTBREAD BARS
Serves 10

A good way to stay positive in life is to derive joy from small, everyday things—like the heavenly scent of these bars in the oven and the buttery-delicious taste when they're done. As if filled with butter and sugar, these magically healthy bars somehow make ordinary life extraordinary.

---

1 cup cashew butter (to make, just blend about 2 cups cashews until smooth)
¼ cup dark honey
1 tbsp almond butter
½ cup vanilla protein powder (can sub oat flour)
¼ cup flaxseed meal
2 tsp vanilla
¼ cup dried blueberries

Mix all ingredients together. Press firmly into an 8x8 baking dish lined with aluminum foil. Pop in the freezer for 30 minutes to an hour.

Remove from freezer and cut into bars. If you'd prefer these bars raw, go ahead and just pop them back into the refrigerator or freezer until you're ready to eat them. If you'd like to bake them and get the texture of shortbread, preheat oven to 300°F. Place on cookie sheet and bake for 20 minutes. Enjoy!

Serving size (46g = 1 bar)
Amount per serving: Calories 230, % Daily Value, Total Fat 15g - 19%, Saturated Fat 3g - 15%, Trans Fat 0g, Cholesterol 10mg - 3%, Sodium 95mg - 4%, Total Carbohydrate 19g - 7%, Dietary Fiber 2g - 7%, Total Sugars 11g, Added Sugars8g -16%, Protein 7g, Vitamin D 0mcg - 0%, Calcium 7mg - 2%, Iron 2mg - 10%, Potassium 153mg - 4%

SANDWICHES & SMALL PLATES

ALMOND BUTTER SWEET POTATO TOAST
Serves 1

A crusty piece of whole wheat toast is a simple, healthy pleasure in itself, but it is best to keep the diet varied and have some equally delicious alternatives on hand. Here, sweet potato takes a page out of bread's book and hops in the toaster to become the root vegetable equivalent of a slice of bread. In doing so, it brings to life that age old phrase "the best thing since sliced bread."

---

2 sweet potato slices
2 tbsp almond butter
½ banana, sliced
Optional toppings: sprinkle of cinnamon, sesame seeds, dark honey drizzle

---

Slice sweet potato lengthwise into 1/4-inch slices. Pop 2 slices into the toaster and toast, just like you would slices of bread. You'll know they are done when they begin to brown on the sides. Toast 'em 2-3 times if necessary depending on your toaster settings.

Top with a luxurious smear of almond butter, banana, and toppings of choice.

Serving size (194g)
Amount per serving: Calories 340, % Daily Value, Total Fat 18g - 23%, Saturated Fat 2g - 10%, Trans Fat 0g, Cholesterol 0mg - 0%, Sodium 95mg - 4%, Total Carbohydrate 42g - 15%, Dietary Fiber 8g - 29%, Total Sugars 18g, Added Sugars 0g - 0%, Protein 9g, Vitamin D 0mcg - 0%, Calcium 136mg - 10%, Iron 2mg - 10%, Potassium 809mg - 15%

SWEET POTATO FALAFELS
Serves 4

Greek-inspired flavors are at the heart of the Mediterranean diet, which traces its origin to Greece and Italy. The diet came to fame in the medical world because of its natural heart-healthy effects. Incidentally, the diet is not just healthy, but also filled with bold flavors and delicious traditional dishes such as these falafels.

---

1 medium raw sweet potato, peeled and cut into chunks
1 cup cooked brown rice and/or quinoa
½ cup almonds
1 egg
1 tsp salt
½ cup whole wheat flour

Add all ingredients to food processor or high-power blender and blend until smooth.

Heat 1 tbsp olive oil in skillet or frying pan over low-medium heat.

Use spoon to drop falafel balls onto skillet.

After about 2 minutes or when bottom is lightly browned, flip to cook the other side for 2 minutes.

Serve on top of Mediterranean Masterpiece salad, in a wrap, or eat on their own with a dollop of hummus.

Serving size (125g)
Amount per serving: Calories 260, % Daily Value, Total Fat 11g - 14%, Saturated Fat 1g - 5%, Trans Fat 0g, Cholesterol 45mg - 15%, Sodium 520mg - 23%, Total Carbohydrate 31g - 11%, Dietary Fiber 6g - 21%, Total Sugars 3g, Added Sugars 0g - 0%, Protein 10g, Vitamin D 1mcg - 6%, Calcium 69mg - 6%, Iron 2mg - 10%, Potassium 367mg - 8%

NOT-SO-SECRET SAUCE SANDWICH

Why should something be secret when it has the potential to bring joy to so many plates and bellies? This sauce is fantastic on just about anything, but it sure is perfect on a sandwich.

---

2 slices of daily bread
1 tbsp not-so-secret sauce

Optional toppings:
turkey
chicken
sliced tomato
sliced cucumber
sliced avocado
Refreshing Arugula Salad
Broccoli sprouts
Pan-fried tofu

Gather your ingredients and prepare the desired veggies, make everything handy.

Slice bread and toast if desired.

Spread perfect spread on one slice of bread. Top with desired toppings and second slice of bread, and enjoy!

Serving size (48g = ~2 tbsp)
Amount per serving: Calories 90, % Daily Value, Total Fat 8g - 10%, Saturated Fat 0.5g - 3%, Trans Fat 0g, Cholesterol 0mg - 0%, Sodium 115mg - 5%, Total Carbohydrate 4g - 1%, Dietary Fiber 1g - 4%, Total Sugars 0g, Added Sugars 0g - 0%, Protein 3g, Vitamin D 0mcg - 0%, Calcium 29mg - 2%, Iron 1mg - 6%, Potassium 60mg - 2%

OPEN FACE CURRIED & CLASSIC CHICKPEA SALAD SANDWICH
Serves 4

This is a delicious alternative to lunchtime favorites such as tuna or chicken salad made with mayonnaise. Here, regular mayo is replaced with either avocado or homemade mayo, which both provide plenty of creaminess and healthy fats.

---

1 15-oz can chickpeas, drained and rinsed
½ medium avocado or ¼ cup make-your-own-mayo
2 tbsp chives, chopped
Salt and pepper

For classic:
⅓ cup celery, chopped
Optional: ⅓ cup cranberries, ½ cup walnuts, ½ cup chopped green apple

For curry:
2 tbsp lemon juice
4 baby dill pickles, chopped

¼ cup chopped fresh parsley
⅓ cup dried currants
¼ tsp turmeric
1 tbsp curry powder

In a medium bowl, mash together chickpeas and avocado/mayo. Stir in chives, salt, and pepper.

Choose your adventure: classic or curry? Add the remainder of the ingredients and mix thoroughly.

Spread on a slice of daily bread, and there you have a delicious, filling, healthy lunch! Store in the fridge to make sandwiches or put a big spoonful on top of salads for the rest of the week.

Serving size (211g)
Amount per serving: Calories 260, % Daily Value, Total Fat 6g - 8%, Saturated Fat 0.5g - 3%, Trans Fat 0g, Cholesterol 0mg - 0%, Sodium 460mg - 20%, Total Carbohydrate 44g - 16%, Dietary Fiber 9g - 32%, Total Sugars 1g, Added Sugars 1g - 2%, Protein 11g, Vitamin D 0mcg - 0%, Calcium 59mg - 4%, Iron 3mg - 15%, Potassium 416mg - 8%

MAKE-YOUR-OWN MAYO

There are a handful of recipes in which mayo is an absolute star. This recipe shines brightest because of its wonderful olive oil base, providing good, unsaturated fats that both anatomical and metaphorical hearts love.

---

1 cup olive oil
½ cup unsweetened soy milk
2 tsp apple cider vinegar
Salt to taste

Place all the ingredients except oil in a blender blend for a few seconds. Now keep the blender on low and add the oil gradually. Turn blender gradually from low to high and blend until thickened.

Taste and add more salt if needed. If it's too thick, add more soy milk. If it's too watery, add more oil.

Serving size (14g = ~1 tbsp)
Amount per serving: Calories 80, % Daily Value, Total Fat 9g – 12%, Saturated Fat 1g – 5%, Trans Fat 0g, Cholesterol 0mg – 0%, Sodium 0mg – 0%, Total Carbohydrate 0g – 0%, Dietary Fiber 0g – 0%, Total Sugars 0g, Added Sugars 0g – 0%, Protein 0g, Vitamin D 0mcg – 0%, Calcium 1mg – 0%, Iron 0mg – 0%, Potassium 6mg – 0%

CRISPY SALMON CAKES
Serves 4

Salmon cakes give the experience of a fancy dish at an expensive restaurant. Though "fancy" and "expensive" are in no way synonymous with good taste and nutrition, sometimes an artfully plated dish and a special location are important parts of a positive experience of food. This recipe provides a bit of that same joy right at home.

---

1 15-oz can salmon
2 eggs
2 tbsp almond flour
6 green onions, finely chopped
½ cup parsley, chopped
½ tsp cumin
½ tsp garlic powder
2 tsp nutritional yeast (optional)
¼ cup lemon juice
2 tsp Dijon mustard
¼ tsp salt
¼ tsp pepper

Mix all ingredients together in a medium bowl. Form into 9 small patties.

Heat a skillet (nonstick or sprayed with nonstick spray) over medium heat. Place patties on skillet and cook for 5 minutes on each side.

Serve over Refreshing Arugula Salad with a sprinkle of cheese or nutritional yeast on top.

Serving size (180g)
Amount per serving: Calories 220, % Daily Value, Total Fat 9g - 12%, Saturated Fat 1.5g - 8%, Trans Fat 0g, Cholesterol 175mg - 58%, Sodium 590mg - 26%, Total Carbohydrate 4g - 1%, Dietary Fiber 1g - 4%, Total Sugars 1g, Added Sugars 0g - 0%, Protein 31g, Vitamin D 16mcg - 80%, Calcium 97mg - 8%, Iron 2mg - 10%, Potassium 457mg - 10%

MEDITERRANEAN STUFFED PEPPERS
Serves 6

This dish is surprisingly filling, and it's a resourceful way to reuse the spiced cauliflower rice recipe. Try making a double batch of spiced cauliflower rice, using it as a side dish one day, and then making these vibrant stuffed peppers the next. It is always nice to plan ahead and find little ways to simplify, simplify, simplify.

---

6 bell peppers
¼ tsp crushed red pepper flakes
½ cup cherry tomatoes, quartered
6 tbsp low-fat feta cheese
1 batch spiced cauliflower rice

Make Spiced Cauliflower Rice (see recipe). Transfer to a large bowl and stir in red pepper flakes and tomatoes.

Cut off the tops of the peppers. Scoop, cut, and wash out the seeds as best you can.

Place the pepper cups open side up on a baking sheet and broil for 3 minutes. Turn them over and broil for an additional 5-7 minutes, until the skin is slightly charred.

Scoop the tabbouleh into the peppers. Top each with 1 tbsp crumbled feta, then broil for an additional 3-5 minutes until the cheese has browned.

Serving size (272g)
Amount per serving: Calories 90, % Daily Value, Total Fat 3g - 4%, Saturated Fat 0.5g - 3%, Trans Fat 0g, Cholesterol 5mg - 2%, Sodium 400mg - 17%, Total Carbohydrate 13g - 5%, Dietary Fiber 5g - 18%, Total Sugars 6g, Added Sugars 0g - 0%, Protein 7g, Vitamin D 0mcg - 0%, Calcium 113mg - 8%, Iron 1mg - 6%, Potassium 553mg - 10%

BALANCE BOWLS
Serves 4

Balance is an oft-pursued state of being and a life-long journey. Healthy eating has substantial effects on overall health and balance, from the meditative act of cooking to the nourishment of the food itself. These bowls are a metaphor for a balanced life—a perfect complement of colors, flavors, and textures in a bowl. Make a batch or two on a Sunday and pack it in jars for an easy lunch and grounding dose of balance throughout the week.

For bowl:
1 tbsp olive oil
1 medium sweet potato, cut into cubes
2 beets, skinned and cubed
1 15-oz can chickpeas, drained and rinsed
2 tsp chili powder
1 tsp salt
2 cups kale, chopped
Cooked quinoa or brown rice
1 avocado, sliced

For sauce:
¼ cup water
¼ cup tahini
1 tsp turmeric
1 clove garlic
¼ tsp salt

Preheat oven to 450°F. Add sweet potato and beets to a baking sheet lined with aluminum foil. Add olive oil and salt and mix thoroughly.

Now add chickpeas to the pan if there's room, otherwise use a different baking sheet. Rub chickpeas with chili powder. Pop in the oven and bake for 20 minutes.

Meanwhile, cook quinoa or rice and make sauce. Add all sauce ingredients to a blender and blend until smooth.

To assemble, layer rice or quinoa, roasted beets and sweet potato, fresh kale, chili chickpeas, and avocado.

*not including quinoa or rice
Serving size (289g)
Amount per serving: Calories 350, % Daily Value, Total Fat 20g - 26%, Saturated Fat 2.5g - 13%, Trans Fat 0g, Cholesterol 0mg - 0%, Sodium 1030mg - 45%, Total Carbohydrate 37g - 13%, Dietary Fiber 10g - 36%, Total Sugars 6g, Added Sugars 0g - 0%, Protein 11g, Vitamin D 0mcg - 0%, Calcium 97mg - 8%, Iron 4mg - 20%Potassium 795mg - 15%

VEGGIE SPICE QUESADILLAS
Serves 6

With the influence of its neighbor Mexico, San Diego inspires healthy versions of classic dishes that still honor the culture and heart of traditional Mexican food. These quesadillas are light and perfect for a lunch that provides a little midday spice to liven up the day.

For veggies:
- 1 tsp ground cumin
- 1 tsp paprika
- ¼ tsp ground black pepper
- ¼ tsp chili powder
- ¼ tsp garlic powder
- ¼ tsp salt
- 1 bell pepper sliced into strips
- 1 small zucchini or yellow squash diced or cut into quarter-moons
- 1 small red onion thinly sliced

For avocado:
- 1 avocado, mashed
- ½ lime, juiced
- salt and pepper

For serving:
- 6 whole wheat flour tortillas
- 1 16-oz can black beans
- Salsa

Chop your veggies and place in a large bowl. Add spices to the veggies and toss thoroughly. Heat a few tbsp water over low-medium heat. Add veggies and cook until softened, about 10 minutes. Remove from heat.

Mash your avocado and mix in lime juice, salt, and pepper.

To assemble, lay out tortillas and fill half with layers of beans, avocado mash, and veggies. Fold in half to make a half-moon-shaped quesadilla. Toast each side for about 3 minutes on a skillet over low-medium heat. Serve with salsa or maybe even some queso or Cilantro Crema!

Serving size (199g)
Amount per serving: Calories 250, % Daily Value, Total Fat 8g - 10%, Saturated Fat 1.5g - 8%, Trans Fat 0g, Cholesterol 0mg - 0%, Sodium 500mg - 22%, Total Carbohydrate 41g - 15%, Dietary Fiber 7g - 25%, Total Sugars 2g, Added Sugars 0g - 0%, Protein 9g, Vitamin D 0mcg - 0%, Calcium 48mg - 4%, Iron 2mg - 10%, Potassium 524mg - 10%

SALADS & SIDE DISHES

REFRESHING ARUGULA SALAD
Serves 2

Sophisticated in its simplicity, this salad is the perfect companion for any dish—a refreshing daily dose of greens adorned with an understated dressing of salt, pepper, olive oil, and lemon juice. It is also a clever way to add greens to a sandwich, or it could serve as a nice, leafy bed on which to plate salmon or kabocha squash.

---

3 cups arugula
1 tsp olive oil
1 tbsp shaved Parmesan
Half lemon, juiced (can replace with a tablespoon of balsamic vinegar if preferred)
Salt and pepper

Clean and dry arugula. Sprinkle with salt, pepper, and shaved parmesan.

Add olive oil and lemon juice. Toss, and serve!

—◇◇—

Serving size (56g)
Amount per serving: Calories 45, % Daily Value, Total Fat 3.5g - 4%, Saturated Fat 1g - 5%, Trans Fat 0g, Cholesterol 5mg - 2%, Sodium 65mg - 3%, Total Carbohydrate 2g - 1%, Dietary Fiber 1g - 4%, Total Sugars 1g, Added Sugars 0g - 0%, Protein 2g, Vitamin D 0mcg - 0%, Calcium 113mg - 8%, Iron 1mg - 6%, Potassium 8mg - 0%

MEDITERRANEAN MASTERPIECE SALAD
Serves 2

This hearty salad favorite is full of flavor and all kinds of filling ingredients that will satisfy even the hungriest family member or friend. The recipe lives up to its name, transforming a salad into a museum-worthy work of art.

---

3 cups choice of leafy greens (kale is heartier and lasts longer for leftovers)
½ cup cherry tomatoes, sliced in half
½ cup cucumber, sliced and cut into quarters
8 Sweet Potato Falafels (see recipe)
2 tbsp Everyday Hummus (see recipe)
Optional add-ins: ⅓ cup canned artichoke hearts, ⅓ cup Greek olives, ¼ cup sun-dried tomatoes, ⅓ cup avocado, 1 tbsp feta cheese, Crispy Seared Tofu, stuffed grape leaves
1 tsp olive oil
Half lemon, juiced (can replace with a tablespoon of balsamic vinegar if preferred)
Salt and pepper

Put all ingredients into a large salad bowl, and make it look amazing.

Dress with salt, pepper, olive oil, and lemon juice.

—◇◇—

Serving size (300g)
Amount per serving: Calories 380, % Daily Value, Total Fat 19g - 24%, Saturated Fat 2g - 10%, Trans Fat 0g, Cholesterol 45mg - 15%, Sodium 660mg - 29%, Total Carbohydrate 43g - 16%, Dietary Fiber 10g - 36%, Total Sugars 5g, Added Sugars 0g - 0%, Protein 14g, Vitamin D 1mcg 6%, Calcium 140mg - 0%, Iron 4mg - 20%, Potassium 738mg - 15%

CRISPY SEARED TOFU
Serves 4

Making a salad into a main dish requires a variety of ingredients, flavors, and textures. Crispy on the outside and juicy on the inside, a few pieces of pan-fried tofu are a quick and easy way to add warm and filling protein to a salad.

---

1 16-ounce package of firm or extra firm tofu
1 tbsp olive oil
Salt and pepper

Heat olive oil over high heat on a skillet or frying pain.

Cut slab of tofu into medium-sized pieces. Use paper towels to gently soak up as much of the water from the tofu as possible.

Place tofu on skillet. Sprinkle the tops with salt and pepper. Once the bottoms are browned and crispy, about 1-2 minutes, flip over using a spatula and cook the other side an additional 1-2 minutes.

Hot from the pan, serve on top of the Magnificent Mediterranean or White Bean & Kale salads!

Serving size (300g)
Amount per serving: Calories 380, % Daily Value, Total Fat 19g - 24%, Saturated Fat 2g - 10%, Trans Fat 0g, Cholesterol 45mg - 15%, Sodium 660mg - 29%, Total Carbohydrate 43g - 16%, Dietary Fiber 10g - 36%, Total Sugars 5g, Added Sugars 0g - 0%, Protein 14g, Vitamin D 1mcg - 6%, Calcium 140mg10 - %, Iron 4mg20 - %, Potassium 738m - 15%

WHITE BEAN & KALE SALAD
Serves 2

Any number of ingredients can come together and call themselves a salad, but only once in a while does a salad achieve a certain perfection of flavor as does this recipe. There's just something about this combination that is truly special.

---

3 cups kale, chopped
⅓ cup white beans
½ avocado, chopped
2 tbsp toasted pine nuts
1 tbsp shaved parmesan cheese
Optional add-ons: 2 5-oz oven-roasted salmon filets, Crispy Seared Tofu, Beyond Meat grilled chicken
1 tsp olive oil
½ lemon, juiced

Place chopped kale into a medium bowl and massage with your hands to soften.

Add white beans, chopped avocado, pine nuts, parmesan cheese, and our simple dressing (olive oil and lemon). Toss, and serve!

Serving size (300g)
Amount per serving: Calories 380, % Daily Value, Total Fat 19g - 24%, Saturated Fat 2g - 10%, Trans Fat 0g, Cholesterol 45mg - 15%, Sodium 660mg - 29%, Total Carbohydrate 43g - 16%, Dietary Fiber 10g - 36%, Total Sugars 5g, Added Sugars 0g - 0%, Protein 14g, Vitamin D 1mcg - 6%, Calcium 140mg - 10%, Iron 4mg - 20%, Potassium 738mg - 15%

ROASTED VEGGIE SALAD WITH CREAMY AVOCADO DRESSING
Serves 4

Here is an easy recipe where the main event is roasting a bunch of vegetables. Once they are situated in the oven, the chef is free to relax while dinner is busy becoming delicious. Then, nutrient-dense avocado dressing swoops in to transform this colorful salad into a filling main dish.

---

1 red bell pepper, sliced
1 ½ cups butternut squash, cut into bite size squares
4 cups Brussels sprouts, hulled and halved
2 tsp dried oregano
½ tsp salt
1 tsp black pepper
3 tbsp olive oil
4 cups mixed greens
Sprinkle of sunflower seeds (optional)

For dressing:
1 avocado
1 clove garlic
1 lime, juiced
¼ cup olive oil
¼ tsp salt
¼ tsp black pepper

Preheat oven to 400°F.

In a large bowl, toss butternut squash, bell pepper, brussel sprouts, dried oregano, salt, pepper, and olive oil until coated. Pour onto an aluminum foil-lined baking sheet and roast for 40 minutes.

Meanwhile, blend the avocado, garlic, lime juice, salt, and pepper in a blender or food processor until creamy. While blending on low, slowly pour in olive oil until the mixture is light and fluffy.

To serve, top greens with roasted vegetables, spoon on the dressing, and sprinkle with sunflower seeds.

Serving size (307g)
Amount per serving: Calories 370, % Daily Value, Total Fat 30g - 38%, Saturated Fat 4g - 20%, Trans Fat 0g, Cholesterol 0mg - 0%, Sodium 410mg - 18%, Total Carbohydrate 25g - 9%, Dietary Fiber 8g - 29%, Total Sugars 5g, Added Sugars 0g - 0%, Protein 7g, Vitamin D 0mcg - 0%, Calcium 137mg - 10%, Iron 4mg - 20%, Potassium 1022mg - 20%

HEARTY ROASTED KABOCHA SQUASH
Serves 4

This kabocha squash recipe serves up a savory winter squash with a melt-in-your-mouth inner texture and a crispy outer skin—a warming companion to a salad or main dish.

---

1 kabocha squash
¼ cup olive oil
1 tbsp Italian seasoning blend (basil, oregano, rosemary, thyme)
Optional cheese (regular or vegan mozzarella)

Preheat oven to 400°F.

Wash kabocha squash thoroughly and carefully cut into 8 slices, continuing to cut the squash in half until you have 8 slices. Place slices on a baking sheet lined with aluminum foil.

Brush or drizzle each slice with a little olive oil, about 2 tsp each or until the orange surface is lightly coated. Sprinkle each slice with Italian seasoning blend, about 1 tsp per slice. If desired, sprinkle with regular or vegan mozzarella, about 2 tsp per slice.

Bake for 40 minutes or until slices are easily pierced with a fork. Serve atop or alongside a salad, and don't forget—you can eat the skin, too!

Serving size (242g)
Amount per serving: Calories 200, % Daily Value, Total Fat 13g - 17%, Saturated Fat 2g - 10%, Trans Fat 0g, Cholesterol 0mg - 0%, Sodium 0mg - 0%, Total Carbohydrate 19g - 7%, Dietary Fiber 3g - 11%, Total Sugars 8g, Added Sugars 0g - 0%, Protein 3g, Vitamin D 0mcg - 0%, Calcium 53mg - 4%, Iron 1mg - 6%, Potassium 30mg - 0%

KALE CAESAR SALAD WITH BLACKENED TEMPEH
Serves 4

Packed full of nutrients in every nook and cranny, this salad is pure nutritious delicious. Blackened tempeh may sound like the unattainable crown jewel of a salad, but it is actually as easy as blending spices together and toasting up some tempeh on the stove.

For dressing:
- ½ cup cashews
- ¼ cup water
- 2 tbsp olive oil
- 1 tbsp lemon juice
- ½ tbsp mustard (spicy brown/Dijon)
- ½ tsp garlic powder
- 1 clove garlic, minced or pressed
- 3 tsp capers
- ½ tsp salt

For tempeh:
- 16 oz (2 8-oz packages) tempeh
- ¼ tsp garlic powder
- ¼ tsp onion powder
- 1 tsp chili powder
- 1 tsp salt
- 1 tsp smoked paprika
- 1 tsp cumin
- 1 pinch black pepper

For salad:
- 4 cups kale, chopped
- Optional add-ins: avocado, shaved parmesan, capers

Cut tempeh into small triangles. Place in a steaming basket over 1 inch of boiling water, cover, and steam for 10 minutes.

Meanwhile, prepare spice mixture by whisking spices together thoroughly in a small bowl.

When tempeh is ready, heat a large skillet (nonstick or sprayed) over medium heat. Press each side of the tempeh into the spice mixture and add to pan. Cook each side for 4-5 minutes, until darkened.

While tempeh is blackening, prepare dressing. Add all ingredients to a blender and blend until smooth.

Add kale, tempeh, and any add-ins to a large bowl. Drizzle dressing and serve!

Serving size (167g)
Amount per serving: Calories 380, % Daily Value, Total Fat 26g - 33%, Saturated Fat 5g - 25%, Trans Fat 0g, Cholesterol 0mg - 0%, Sodium 920mg - 40%, Total Carbohydrate 17g - 6%, Dietary Fiber 2g - 7%, Total Sugars 2g, Added Sugars 0g - 0%, Protein 27g, Vitamin D 0mcg - 0%, Calcium 175mg - 15%, Iron 5mg - 30%, Potassium 606mg - 15%

TENDER SAUTÉED GREENS
Serves 4

Raw greens transform into a warming, versatile side dish in just five minutes with this recipe. The more ways to incorporate greens into the diet, the merrier!

---

3 tbsp olive oil
3 cloves garlic, minced
¼ tsp red chili flakes
1 lb kale, chopped
Salt and pepper

Heat oil over low heat in a large pot or Dutch oven. Sauté garlic and chili flakes until garlic begins to brown, about 2 minutes. Careful not to burn the garlic!

Add the kale and toss. The pot will be full, but don't worry—the kale will shrink big-time. Cover and allow to cook for 5 minutes.

Toss in salt and pepper and continue cooking for 3 minutes, or until greens have shrunk in size, stirring as needed.

Serve as a vibrant green side to any dish!

———◇◇———

Serving size (124g)
Amount per serving: Calories 150, % Daily Value, Total Fat 11g - 14%, Saturated Fat 1.5g - 8%, Trans Fat 0g, Cholesterol 0mg - 0%, Sodium 45mg - 2%, Total Carbohydrate 10g - 4%, Dietary Fiber 4g - 14%, Total Sugars 3g, Added Sugars 0g - 0%, Protein 5g, Vitamin D 0mcg - 0%, Calcium 170mg - 15%, Iron 2mg - 10%, Potassium 559mg - 10%

SPICED CAULIFLOWER RICE
Serves 2

In many cultures, rice is a staple in every meal. Rice itself is a wonderful whole grain, but this version of rice is actually a heaping plate of vegetables. Clever cauliflower strikes again to provide a delicious alternative that helps keep the diet varied.

---

16 oz cauliflower, riced
1 tbsp olive oil
3 cloves garlic, minced
½ tsp salt
2 tsp parsley, chopped
1 tsp lemon juice

Preheat oven to 425°F.

Place cauliflower into food processor or high-power blender and blend until you get the texture of rice. Or just use an already-prepared bag of riced cauliflower!

Line a sheet pan with aluminum foil. Add cauliflower and remaining ingredients straight to the baking sheet, toss to mix, and spread out.

Bake for 25 minutes, giving it a little mix at the halfway point. Remove from the oven and that's all folks!

Serving size (243g)
Amount per serving: Calories 120, % Daily Value, Total Fat 7g - 9%, Saturated Fat 1g - 5%, Trans Fat 0g, Cholesterol 0mg - 0%, Sodium 550mg - 24%, Total Carbohydrate 13g - 5%, Dietary Fiber 5g - 18%, Total Sugars 4g, Added Sugars 0g - 0%, Protein 5g, Vitamin D 0mcg - 0%, Calcium 60mg - 4%, Iron 1mg 6%, Potassium 706mg - 15%

CURRIED CAULIFLOWER QUINOA
Serves 10

This recipe makes a large batch for a good reason: leftovers. Carefully tested by countless friends and family members over the years, it has become clear that the marriage of curry spice and creamy texture in this dish never disappoints nor does it ever get old. Make it as a side dish or serve atop a salad for a light dinner or lunches throughout the week.

---

16 oz (~2 ½ cups) quinoa
1 head cauliflower, broken into pieces (I prefer more cauliflower, such as large head or a 24-oz bag of cauliflower florets)
1 tbsp curry powder
1 tbsp turmeric
1 tbsp cumin
1 tbsp coriander
1 ½ tsp salt
¼- ½ tsp cayenne pepper
3 tbsp light brown sugar
3 tbsp olive oil
3 medium-sized carrots, peeled and diced
1 cup Make-Your-Own Mayo
½ lime, juiced

Preheat oven to 450°F. In a small bowl, mix spices & olive oil. Directly on the baking sheet, toss the cauliflower and carrots with the oil-spice. Roast in the oven until cauliflower is browned around the edges but still crunchy, about 20 minutes.

Meanwhile, while the veggies are a-roasting, cook the quinoa.

When veggies are finished, remove from oven and add to a large bowl with the quinoa. Fold in the mayo and lime juice. Enjoy freshly made and warm or after chilling in the refrigerator!

Serving size (167g)
Amount per serving: Calories 380, % Daily Value, Total Fat 22g - 28%, Saturated Fat 2.5g - 13%, Trans Fat 0g, Cholesterol 0mg - 0%, Sodium 340mg - 15%, Total Carbohydrate 43g - 16%, Dietary Fiber 6g - 21%, Total Sugars 6g, Added Sugars 4g - 8%, Protein 8g, Vitamin D 0mcg - 0%, Calcium 60mg - 4%, Iron 5mg - 30%, Potassium 649mg - 15%

MAIN DISHES & ENTREES

CALIFORNIA QUINOA BOWL WITH NOT-SO-SECRET SAUCE
Serves 12

Quinoa is a wonderful alternative to rice or pasta because it has more protein and fiber. It is actually a perfect protein, meaning it contains all the essential amino acids in one. That's pretty amazing for one little plant! As for this quinoa-based bowl, there's something about this unexpected combination of sauce ingredients that lends shockingly savory and delicious cohesion to this Southwestern-inspired bowl... and pretty much anything else.

For sauce:	For bowl:
½ cup water	Cooked quinoa
½ cup lemon juice	Black Beans
¼ cup canola oil	Kidney beans
½ cup almond meal	Tomatoes
⅓ cup nutritional yeast	Avocado
½ cup cooked chickpeas	Black olives
⅓ cup tofu	Shredded cheddar
2 cloves garlic, minced	Salsa
½ tsp salt	
1 ½ tsp curry powder	
1 tsp dried oregano	
1 tsp cilantro	

To make the sauce, add all ingredients to a blender and blend until smooth.

To assemble the bowls, add cooked quinoa to the bottom. Then add black beans, kidney beans, tomato, avocado, olives, and a sprinkle of cheddar and drizzle (or douse?) with sauce.

Note: *To make quinoa that is fluffy and al dente, 1 ½ cups quinoa (or however much you need—you don't even have to measure with this recipe) to a large pot of salted boiling water. Boil for 10-12 minutes, stirring occasionally. Drain quinoa in a mesh colander, and it's ready to use as a base for quinoa bowls, in sweet potato falafels, or on top of a salad!*

Serving size (48g = ~2 tbsp)
Amount per serving: Calories 90, % Daily Value, Total Fat 8g - 10%, Saturated Fat 0.5g - 3%, Trans Fat 0g, Cholesterol 0mg - 0%, Sodium 115mg - 5%, Total Carbohydrate 4g - 1%, Dietary Fiber 1g - 4%, Total Sugars 0g, Added Sugars 0g - 0%, Protein 3g, Vitamin D 0mcg - 0%, Calcium 29mg - 2%, Iron 1mg - 6%, Potassium 60mg - 2%

MOROCCAN BROCCOLI & TOFU QUINOA BOWL
Serves 4

This is one of those "chop, roast, and done" recipes that makes for an easy dinner anytime. Harissa paste might seem like an exotic, elusive ingredient, but it can actually be found on the shelves of a neighborhood market, and it adds a unique burst of Moroccan flavor and spice. A little jar of it lasts forever in the fridge, where it will remain perfectly poised to make this dish again and again.

---

1 16-ounce package extra firm tofu,
1 large head of broccoli, broken into florets
½ red onion, cut into large slices
1 ½ cups quinoa
2 tbsp harissa paste
¼ cup olive oil
3 tbsp apple cider vinegar
Salt and pepper
Sliced avocado for serving

Preheat oven to 425°F. Line a large baking sheet with aluminum foil.

Place tofu on a cutting board with a couple layers of paper towel on top. Put a plate on top of the paper towels and press to squeeze water out of the tofu.

Mix harissa, ¼ cup oil, and 3 tbsp vinegar cup and set aside.

Place broccoli, tofu, and red onion straight onto the baking sheet. Pour harissa mixture over the top, and sprinkle with salt and pepper. Toss mixture with your hands until well coated.

Bake for 30-40 minutes, until lightly browned and crispy.

To serve, divide quinoa into bowls. Top with tofu-broccoli mixture and a couple slices of avocado.

*Serving size (242g) *not including avocado*
Amount per serving: Calories 400, % Daily Value, Total Fat 20g - 26%, Saturated Fat 2.5g - 13%, Trans Fat 0g, Cholesterol 0mg - 0%, Sodium 95mg - 4%, Total Carbohydrate 43g - 16%, Dietary Fiber 6g - 21%, Total Sugars 3g, Added Sugars 0g - 0%, Protein 16g, Vitamin D 0mcg - 0%, Calcium 168mg - 15%, Iron 6mg - 35%, Potassium 668mg - 15%

TWICE-BAKED SANTA FE SWEET POTATOES WITH CILANTRO CREMA
Serves 3

Simple, baked sweet potato is in itself a creamy, buttery package of perfection, but adding savory southwestern flavors makes for a filling, warming, and delightful dish.

---

3 sweet potatoes
1 tsp cumin
1 tsp turmeric
¼ tsp chili powder
A few dashes of garlic powder
A few dashes of onion powder
Salt and pepper
¾ cup black beans
¾ cup corn
3 tbsp low-fat or vegan shredded cheddar
Toppings: avocado, bell pepper, white onion, and chopped pasilla chili

---

Either bake or microwave sweet potatoes until soft. Preheat oven to 400°F.

Once slightly cooled, scoop out insides and put into bowl. Mash lightly.

Add spices, black beans, and corn and stir. Put mixture back into sweet potato skins and sprinkle with a tablespoon of low-fat cheddar.

Return to oven and bake 15-20 minutes. Remove from oven and add desired toppings, a drizzle of cilantro crema, and serve!

Serving size (267g)
Amount per serving: Calories 220, % Daily Value, Total Fat 1.5g - 2%, Saturated Fat 0g - 0%, Trans Fat 0g, Cholesterol 0mg - 0%, Sodium 410mg - 18%, Total Carbohydrate 44g - 16%, Dietary Fiber 10g - 36%, Total Sugars 10g, Added Sugars 0g - 0%, Protein 9g, Vitamin D 0mcg - 0%, Calcium 110mg - 8%, Iron 3mg - 15%, Potassium 750mg - 15%

CILANTRO CREMA
Serves 12

Although there is technically no cream, that doesn't mean this crema can't be creamy! It's the perfect drizzle for twice-baked sweet potatoes, black bean burgers, quesadillas, and nachos.

¾ cup cashews
½ cup fresh cilantro leaves
1 clove garlic
½ cup water
3 tbsp lime juice
½ tsp salt
½ tsp garlic powder

Add all ingredients to a high-power blender or food processor and blend until smooth. There you have it, folks!

Serving size (23g = 2 tbsp)
Amount per serving: Calories 40, % Daily Value, Total Fat 3g - 4%, Saturated Fat 0.5g - 3%, Trans Fat 0g, Cholesterol 0mg - 0%, Sodium 80mg - 3%, Total Carbohydrate 3g - 1%, Dietary Fiber 0g - 0%, Total Sugars 1g, Added Sugars 0g - 0%, Protein 1g, Vitamin D 0mcg - 0%, Calcium 7mg - 0%, Iron 0mg - 0%, Potassium 14mg - 0%

SAN DIEGO BLACK BEAN BURGER STACKS
Serves 4

These favorite black bean burgers, which bear San Diego's namesake and cultural flavor influences, are easy to make and perfect for grilling or cooking in a pan. These can be enjoyed on a whole wheat burger bun, but they are especially delicious served over lettuce with all kinds of delicious toppings stacked on top, eaten with a knife and fork.

---

1 15-oz can black beans, drained and rinsed
¼ cup old-fashioned rolled oats
¼ cup whole wheat flour
¾ tsp cumin
½ tsp cayenne pepper
½ tsp garlic powder
½ tsp salt
¼ cup chunky salsa

For serving:
Lettuce
Squeeze of lemon or lime
Sliced tomato
Red onion, thinly sliced
Sliced avocado
Vegan mayo
Cilantro crema
Salsa
Low-fat or vegan shredded cheddar

Add black beans to a medium bowl and partially mash with a fork.

Add the rest of the ingredients and mix thoroughly.

Using your hands, form 4 medium-sized patties.

Heat a skillet or frying pan (nonstick or sprayed with nonstick spray) over medium heat. Add patties and cook for about 5 minutes per side.

To serve, add greens to a plate. Squeeze a little lemon or lime on top. Add black bean burger and spread a little mayo on top. Layer on sliced tomato, avocado, red onion, a drizzle of cilantro crema, a dollop of salsa, and a sprinkle of shredded cheddar.

---

*Serving size (137g = 1 large patty) *not including toppings*
Amount per serving: Calories 140, % Daily Value, Total Fat 1g - 1%, Saturated Fat 0g - 0%, Trans Fat 0g, Cholesterol 0mg - 0%, Sodium 500mg - 22%, Total Carbohydrate 29g - 11%, Dietary Fiber 9g - 32%, Total Sugars 2g, Added Sugars 0g - 0%, Protein 8g, Vitamin D 0mcg - 0%, Calcium 60mg - 4%, Iron 2mg - 10%, Potassium 502mg - 10%

CHINESE FRIED RICE
Serves 4

Here is a comforting bowl of fried rice that uses cauliflower rice as a base, a welcome change of pace that sneaks extra veggies into a seemingly indulgent meal. This dish provides all the satisfaction of fried rice from the favorite local Chinese restaurant but with much more nutrition and health benefits.

---

2 eggs, lightly beaten
2 cloves garlic, minced or pressed
2 tsp fresh ginger, peeled and grated
1 cup frozen mixed peas and carrots, thawed
3 scallions, thinly sliced
3 cups cauliflower, riced (made in food processor or prepackaged)
2 tbsp low-sodium soy sauce
2 tbsp toasted sesame oil
1 16-oz package of tofu OR 1 cooked boneless skinless chicken breast, diced

---

Place tofu on a cutting board with a couple layers of paper towel on top. Put a plate on top of the paper towels and press to squeeze water out of the tofu. Cut into small cubes.

Heat a large skillet or frying pan (nonstick or sprayed) over medium-high heat. Add tofu and fry until lightly browned on all sides. Set aside.

Add egg to the same skillet, scramble, and set aside.

Add garlic and ginger to the same skillet, and cook, stirring constantly, for 1 minute.

Add the peas and carrots, cauliflower, soy sauce, sesame oil, and tofu and cook for about 6-7 minutes.

Stir in egg and scallions, and you're ready to serve!

Serving size (283g)
Amount per serving: Calories 270, % Daily Value, Total Fat 17g - 22%, Saturated Fat 3g - 15%, Trans Fat 0g, Cholesterol 90mg - 30%, Sodium 380mg - 17%, Total Carbohydrate 11g - 4%, Dietary Fiber 3g - 11%, Total Sugars 2g, Added Sugars 0g - 0%, Protein 20g, Vitamin D 1mcg - 6%, Calcium 238mg - 20%, Iron 3mg - 15%, Potassium 349mg - 8%

MISO PESTO SOBA NOODLES
Serves 4

This dish has an incredible, unexpected flavor, and packs many nutritious ingredients. With greens galore, miso, and buckwheat, a whole grain, it pushes the boundaries for how much goodness can possibly be contained in one gorgeous green masterpiece-on-a-plate.

---

4 cups spinach
2 cups fresh cilantro
1 tbsp white miso
1 clove garlic
⅓ cup vegetable oil
1 tsp toasted sesame oil
1 tsp lemon juice
10 oz soba noodles
Toasted sesame seeds (for serving)

Cook soba noodles according to package directions.

Meanwhile, add remaining ingredients to a blender and blend until smooth.

Add pesto sauce to noodles and toss. Serve with a sprinkle of toasted sesame seeds and a soft-boiled egg on top. Delicious!

—◇◇—

*Serving size (126g)
Amount per serving: Calories 420, % Daily Value, Total Fat 20g - 26%, Saturated Fat 3g - 15%, Trans Fat 0g, Cholesterol 0mg - 0%, Sodium 700mg - 30%, Total Carbohydrate 56g - 20%, Dietary Fiber 1g - 4%, Total Sugars 1g, Added Sugars 0g - 0%, Protein 11g, Vitamin D 0mcg - 0%, Calcium 47mg - 4%, Iron 3mg - 15%, Potassium 225mg - 4%*

EASY SPLIT PEASY SOUP
Serves 6

Split pea soup is warmth, sustenance, and care in a bowl. There is something undeniably comforting about a big bowl of piping hot split pea soup and a piece of crispy, homemade whole wheat toast on the side for dipping.

---

6 cups vegetable broth
2 cups dried green split peas
1 medium onion, chopped
1 cup carrots, chopped
2 celery ribs, chopped
2 cloves garlic, minced or pressed
½ tsp dried marjoram (oregano works too!)
½ tsp dried basil
¼ tsp cumin
½ tsp salt
¼ tsp pepper

Dump everything into a pot and bring to a boil, turn heat to low and simmer for 1 hour, stirring occasionally.

Serving size (320g)
Amount per serving: Calories 250, % Daily Value, Total Fat 1g - 1%, Saturated Fat 0g - 0%, Trans Fat 0g, Cholesterol 0mg - 0%, Sodium 840mg - 37%, Total Carbohydrate 47g - 17%, Dietary Fiber 17g - 61%, Total Sugars 7g, Added Sugars 0g - 0%, Protein 17g, Vitamin D 0mcg - 0%, Calcium 46mg - 4%, Iron 4mg - 20%, Potassium 654mg - 15%

INDIAN LENTIL DAAL WITH BELL PEPPERS
Serves 6

Each area of India has its own traditional version of daal, so there is a wonderful variety of daals to taste and explore, each telling the story of its own local traditions through flavor. This is a simplified recipe that uniquely incorporates bell peppers for some added vegetables and color.

---

2 cups red or yellow lentils
6 cups water
1 red or yellow bell pepper, chopped
1 red onion, chopped
1 tsp fresh ginger, minced
3 cloves garlic, minced or pressed
½ lemon, juiced
1 tsp turmeric
¾ tsp curry powder
½ tsp cumin
1 tsp ground cilantro
1 pinch cayenne pepper
1 tsp salt

Dump everything into a pot and bring to a boil, turn heat to low and simmer for 30 minutes, stirring occasionally. Serve with brown rice, quinoa, or on its own.

Serving size (359g)
Amount per serving:
Calories 250, % Daily Value, Total Fat 1.5g - 2%, Saturated Fat 0g - 0%, Trans Fat 0g, Cholesterol 0mg - 0%, Sodium 340mg - 15%, Total Carbohydrate 45g - 16%, Dietary Fiber 8g - 29%, Total Sugars 2g, Added Sugars 0g - 0%, Protein 16g, Vitamin D 0mcg - 0%, Calcium 55mg - 4%, Iron 5mg - 30%, Potassium 537mg - 10%

SAAG TOFU "PANEER"
Serves 4

This Indian dish is the ultimate two-step healthy recipe full of greens, tofu, and a warming mix of traditional Indian spices.

---

1 small onion
1 tbsp fresh ginger, minced
3 cloves garlic
9 ounces spinach
1 16-ounce package extra firm tofu, drained and pressed
1 tsp turmeric
1 cup vegetable broth
1 tbsp lemon juice
1 tsp cumin
1 tbsp garam masala
1 tsp chili paste
2 tsp granulated sugar
½ tsp salt
½ cup nonfat Greek yogurt

Heat a nonstick (or sprayed with nonstick spray) pan over medium heat. Cut tofu into medium cubes and add to the pan. Cook tofu until lightly browned on all sides, flipping frequently.

Meanwhile, add remainder of ingredients except Greek yogurt to a high-power blender or food processor. You may need to add the spinach in batches depending on the size of your blender. Blend until mostly but not completely pureed.

Add mixture to the tofu and cook until the liquids evaporate, about 10 minutes. You'll notice the color changes from a bright green to a darker forest green—how pretty! Lastly, stir in the yogurt.

Serve with brown rice or quinoa.

—◇◇—

Serving size (310g)
Amount per serving: Calories 190, % Daily Value, Total Fat 7g - 9%, Saturated Fat 0.5g - 3%, Trans Fat 0g, Cholesterol 0mg - 0%, Sodium 550mg - 24%, Total Carbohydrate 12g - 4%, Dietary Fiber 2g - 7%, Total Sugars 5g, Added Sugars 2g - 4%, Protein 19g, Vitamin D 0mcg - 0%, Calcium 301mg - 25%, Iron 5mg - 30%, Potassium 156mg - 4%

OVEN-ROASTED SALMON
Serves 2

Salmon packs an incredible quantity of healthy fats and nutrients into one delicious parcel and is lower in mercury compared to other fish. It can be intimidating to cook fish, but it is actually quick, easy, and simple to ensure it is properly cooked through. Surprisingly, it is possible to cook what might be a $30 dish at a restaurant for about $5 at home.

---

2 5-oz salmon fillets
Salt and pepper
1 tsp olive oil per fillet (optional, if fish has less natural fat)

Preheat oven to 425°F.

Rub fillets on all sides with salt and pepper. Sometimes (particularly Atlantic salmon) the fish itself has enough fat in it that you don't need additional olive oil, but if it's a dryer piece of fish (wild Alaskan salmon, for example), rub with olive oil.

Be sure to practice safe fish-handling by washing your hands and cooking surfaces!

Place fillets skin side down on a foil-lined baking sheet. Roast until fish is just cooked through, about 12 minutes. To know that the fish is properly cooked, check to see that the flesh in the thickest portion of each fillet is opaque and separates easily with a fork.

Lift salmon flesh from skin with a spatula and serve with a side dish or atop White Bean & Kale Salad.

*Serving size (142g)
Amount per serving: Calories 200, % Daily Value, Total Fat 9g - 12%, Saturated Fat 1.5g - 8%, Trans Fat --g, Cholesterol 80mg - 27%, Sodium 60mg - 3%, Total Carbohydrate 0g - 0%, Dietary Fiber 0g - 0%, Total Sugars 0g, Added Sugars 0g - 0%, Protein 28g, Vitamin D --mcg - --%, Calcium 17mg - 2%, Iron 1mg - 6%, Potassium 695mg - 15%*

KEEN GREEN QUINOA CASSEROLE
Serves 6

A casserole filled with green goodness is a gift, particularly on a Sunday night—not just because casseroles are filling and delicious, but because the inevitable leftovers provide easy, homemade nourishment throughout the week ahead. This recipe has an especially enchanting smell that will leave those within range counting the minutes until that timer goes off.

For casserole:
3 cups chopped kale, packed
3 cups cooked quinoa
2 heaping cups broccoli, chopped
½ cup onion, chopped

For sauce:
1 ½ cups almond milk, soy milk, or low-fat cow's milk
1 15-ounce can cannellini beans, drained and rinsed
¼ cup nutritional yeast
1 tsp black pepper
1 tsp salt
½ tsp fresh thyme (can sub ¼ tsp dried)
½ tsp rosemary (can sub ¼ tsp dried)
A pinch of cayenne

Preheat oven to 375°F. Cook the quinoa.

Meanwhile, add the kale, broccoli, and onion to a 9x13 baking dish.

Blend the sauce ingredients thoroughly in a blender.

Once the quinoa is done, add it to the baking dish. Pour sauce over the casserole mixture and mix thoroughly. Pop in the oven and bake for 40 minutes.

Serving size (228g)
Amount per serving: Calories 200, % Daily Value, Total Fat 2.5g - 3%, Saturated Fat 0g - 0%, Trans Fat 0g, Cholesterol 0mg - 0%, Sodium 460mg - 20%, Total Carbohydrate 35g - 13%, Dietary Fiber 10g - 36%, Total Sugars 2g, Added Sugars 0g - 0%, Protein 11g, Vitamin D 0mcg - 0%, Calcium 99mg - 8%, Iron 3mg - 15%, Potassium 339mg - 8%

QUINOA LASAGNA
Serves 6

Lasagna is one of those soul-satisfying dishes, but it can be heavy, full of cheese and simple carbohydrates. This sneaky recipe swaps lasagna noodles for quinoa and lightens up the traditionally heavy cheeses to make for a more balanced meal that still maintains the soul-satisfying integrity and flavor of a traditional lasagna.

For marinara mixture:
2 cups organic marinara (make sure there's no added sugar!)
2.5 cups vegetable broth
1 cup 1% cottage cheese
1 cup ricotta cheese, low-fat or fat free
1 tbsp Italian seasoning
2 tsp garlic powder
⅛ tsp sea salt
⅛ tsp ground pepper

1 ½ cups quinoa
2 ½ cups cremini mushrooms, diced
4 cups fresh spinach
1 cup yellow onion, diced

For the top:
2 medium tomatoes, sliced
½ cup shredded low-fat mozzarella

Preheat oven to 375°F and spray a 13x9 baking dish with nonstick spray.

Chop your veggies and add them directly to the casserole dish along with the quinoa.

Mix the marinara ingredients in a bowl and pour into the casserole dish. Carefully toss everything together. Cover with aluminum foil and bake for 60 minutes.

Remove from oven and cover the top with sliced tomatoes all lined up in rows, then sprinkle with mozzarella. Pop back in the oven for 5 minutes, then you're done!

Serving size (395g)
Amount per serving: Calories 270, % Daily Value, Total Fat 4g - 5%, Saturated Fat 0g - 0%, Trans Fat 0g, Cholesterol 10mg - 3%, Sodium 990mg - 43%, Total Carbohydrate 39g - 14%, Dietary Fiber 3g - 11%, Total Sugars 9g, Added Sugars 0g - 0%, Protein 19g, Vitamin D 0mcg - 0%, Calcium 243mg - 20%, Iron 4mg - 20%, Potassium 876mg - 20%

ALFREDO PASTA WITH BROCCOLI & SPINACH
Serves 4

Fettucine alfredo is a favorite, classic Italian dish, but it seems to leave a heavy feeling in its wake. This recipe is at once decadent, staying true to the traditional dish, and chock full of vegetables, making it lighter and more nutritious. If using chickpea or whole wheat pasta, try blanching the veggies right in there with the pasta to simplify the process.

---

1 spaghetti squash, chickpea pasta, or whole wheat pasta
1 14-oz package cauliflower florets
3 cups vegetable broth
1 cup almond soy, or 1% milk
2 garlic cloves, minced or pressed
2 heaping cups spinach
1 large head of broccoli, broken into florets
2 tbsp butter or vegan butter
¼ cup nutritional yeast
½ lemon, juiced
½ tsp salt

In a medium pot, boil broth. Add cauliflower and cook about 8 minutes. Remove cauliflower with a slotted spoon and place into blender or food processor.

In a small skillet, heat butter over medium heat and sauté garlic 1-2 minutes. Add to blender along with milk, nutritional yeast, lemon, salt, and pepper and blend.

Meanwhile, boil salted water in a large pot. Add pasta and cook according to package directions. When about halfway finished cooking, add broccoli florets to the pasta pot and continue boiling.

When pasta is about 2 minutes from being done, add spinach to the pasta pot. If you are using spaghetti squash, skip the above steps and steam or sauté your spinach and broccoli instead.

Strain everything in a colander and return to large pot. Add alfredo sauce, mix, and enjoy!

Serving size (902g)
*made with spaghetti squash
Amount per serving: Calories 270, % Daily Value, Total Fat 8g - 10%, Saturated Fat 2.5g - 13%, Trans Fat 0g, Cholesterol 0mg - 0%, Sodium 980mg - 43%, Total Carbohydrate 45g - 16%, Dietary Fiber 12g - 43%, Total Sugars 18g, Added Sugars 0g - 0%, Protein 11g, Vitamin D 1mcg - 6%, Calcium 232mg - 20%, Iron 4mg - 20%, Potassium 1302mg - 30%

PESTO PASTA WITH OVEN-ROASTED TOMATOES
Serves 4

Everybody needs a comforting pasta sometimes... but no body needs a big plate of carbohydrates alone. This recipe is filled with nutrition that will both nourish the body and comfort the soul.

---

1 spaghetti squash (can also use whole wheat pasta or chickpea pasta cooked according to package directions)
1 batch of classic pesto or creamy avocado pesto
1 lb grape tomatoes
2 tbsp olive oil

Preheat oven to 400°F.

Cut spaghetti squash in half longways, place cut side down on an aluminum foil-lined baking sheet and bake for 20-25 minutes. Allow to cool and reduce heat to 350°F.

Drizzle tomatoes with olive oil and season with salt and pepper.

Bake until tomatoes begin to shrivel, 10-15 minutes.

Once squash is cool, remove spaghetti threads with a fork. Scrape the short way, then the long way to scrape threads into a large bowl.

Add desired sauce and toss until combined. Top with roasted tomatoes.

Serving size (648g) *with classic basil presto
Amount per serving: Calories 310, % Daily Value, Total Fat 14g - 18%, Saturated Fat 1.5g - 8%, Trans Fat 0g, Cholesterol 0mg - 0%, Sodium 120mg - 5%, Total Carbohydrate 41g - 15%, Dietary Fiber 9g - 32%, Total Sugars 18g, Added Sugars 0g - 0%, Protein 11g, Vitamin D 0mcg - 0%, Calcium 141mg - 10%, Iron 4mg - 20%, Potassium 1025mg - 20%

Serving size (681g) *with creamy avocado presto
servings per container
Amount per serving: Calories 560, % Daily Value, Total Fat 41g - 53%, Saturated Fat 5g - 25%, Trans Fat 0g, Cholesterol 0mg - 0%, Sodium 250mg - 11%, Total Carbohydrate 48g - 17%, Dietary Fiber 11g - 39%, Total Sugars 17g, Added Sugars 0g - 0%, Protein 12g, Vitamin D 0mcg - 0%, Calcium 110mg - 8%, Iron 4mg - 20%, Potassium 1406mg - 30%

DESSERTS

ELIZABETH EPSTEIN, MD

TAHINI COOKIES
Serves 12

The flavor and nutritional content of tahini adds dimension to all kinds of dishes from appetizers to desserts. Filled with tahini, these soft, pillowy cookies with eye-catching crackled tops provide lasting energy and are more savory than sweet, setting them apart from their cookie-companions and adding a little variety to life.

½ cup tahini
⅓ cup dark honey
¼ tsp vanilla
1 egg
1 ½ cup almond flour
1 tsp baking soda
½ tsp salt
¼ cup sesame seeds (for sprinkling on top)

Preheat oven to 350°F. In a medium bowl, mix all ingredients thoroughly.

Spoon dough onto cookie sheet lined with parchment paper and sprinkle sesame seeds on top. Bake 10-12 minutes.

Serving size (40g = 1 cookie)
Amount per serving: Calories 180, % Daily Value, Total Fat 13g - 17%, Saturated Fat 1.5g - 8%, Trans Fat 0g, Cholesterol 15mg - 5%, Sodium 200mg - 9%, Total Carbohydrate 13g - 5%, Dietary Fiber 2g - 7%, Total Sugars 8g, Added Sugars 8g - 16%, Protein 6g, Vitamin D 0mcg - 0%, Calcium 59mg - 4%, Iron 1mg - 6%, Potassium 58mg - 2%

OATMEAL CHOCOLATE CHIP COOKIES
Serves 21

Oatmeal cookies conjure up the comfort of home. They are a wholesome, kind cookie (if a cookie could be kind), that fills bellies and hearts with goodness. This recipe is special though, taking a step further to fill bellies and hearts with nutritional goodness as well. By replacing butter with almond butter, these cookies create the perfect union of healthy fats with whole grains.

---

1 cup almond butter
2 eggs
1 tsp vanilla
½ cup dark honey
1 ½ cup oats (blended into flour)
1 cup oats (whole)
1 tsp baking soda
½ tsp salt
1 cup dark chocolate chips
Optional: sprinkle of sea salt on top

Preheat oven to 350°F.

Melt the almond butter over the stove or in the microwave if chunky. Skip this step if your almond butter is already nice and smooth. Remove from heat and mix in the eggs, honey, and vanilla.

Add 1 ½ cup oats, baking soda, and salt, to a blender and blend until you have a fine flour. Add flour, remaining 1 cup oats, and chocolate chips to the almond butter mixture and mix thoroughly.

Spoon onto cookie sheet and bake for 15 minutes. Sprinkle with sea salt if desired.

Serving size (43g)
Amount per serving: Calories 190, % Daily Value, Total Fat 11g - 14%, Saturated Fat 3g - 15%, Trans Fat 0g, Cholesterol 15mg - 5%, Sodium 140mg - 6%, Total Carbohydrate 20g - 7%, Dietary Fiber 2g - 7%, Total Sugars 11g, Added Sugars 7g - 14%, Protein 5g, Vitamin D 0mcg - 0%, Calcium 48mg - 4%, Iron 2mg - 10%, Potassium 131mg - 2%

CHOCOLATE CAKE WITH BUTTERLESS CHOCOLATE BUTTERCREAM
Makes 1 layer 8" or 9" pan or a 2-layer 6" cake
Serves 12

Cakes are markers of occasions—birthdays, weddings, holidays, or maybe just a cozy rainy day inside. They can be extravagant or simple and messy, frosting effortlessly lathered over the top, but either way they are something special, and they tend to be a harbinger of joy, contented tummies and souls. But believe it or not, it is possible to make an absolutely delicious and perfect cake healthy, too.

---

1 15-oz can chickpeas, drained and rinsed
1 tsp vanilla
¾ cup granulated sugar
1 ½ tsp baking soda
¼ tsp salt
½ cup dark chocolate chips
3 eggs

Frosting:
1 cup semi-sweet chocolate, chopped (can use chocolate chips)
1 cup dark chocolate, chopped (can use chocolate chips)
½ cup + 2 tbsp canned "lite" coconut milk, room temperature
½ tsp vanilla
1 tsp instant ground espresso powder
4 tbsp canned pumpkin puree
Pinch of salt

Preheat oven to 350°F. Grease pan, and I recommend cutting a piece of parchment paper for the bottom of the pan—it works like a charm for getting the finished cake out smoothly.

In a blender or food processor, blend chickpeas with eggs until smooth.

Add vanilla, sugar, baking soda, and chocolate and blend until smooth. (Though sometimes when I'm lazy I just dump everything in a blender at once and blend—and it's fine!) The batter will have the consistency and look of your everyday chocolate cake batter!

Pour into prepared 9" pan, and bake for 25-30 minutes or until toothpick comes out clean.

Now, make the frosting. Melt chocolate on double boiler or in microwave.

Mix in coconut milk, then vanilla, espresso powder, pumpkin puree, and sea salt. Make sure this mixture is homogenous—if necessary, use a blender. Put in refrigerator to chill.

Once set (~1 hour), use a hand mixer or stand mixer to whip it up. The consistency will be like buttercream!

Serving size (114g = 1 slice)
Amount per serving: Calories 300, % Daily Value, Total Fat 14g - 18%, Saturated Fat 8g - 40%, Trans Fat 0g, Cholesterol 45mg - 15%, Sodium 340mg - 15%, Total Carbohydrate 39g - 14%, Dietary Fiber 3g - 11%, Total Sugars 30g, Added Sugars 20g - 40%, Protein 5g, Vitamin D 1mcg - 6%, Calcium 19mg - 2%, Iron 3mg - 15%, Potassium 106mg - 2%

CHUNKY CHOCOLATE-ALMOND FROZEN YOGURT
Serves 2

Simple ingredients are often full of surprises. Here, bananas undergo transformation in a blender and are reborn as the creamiest frozen yogurt—as if straight from the frozen yogurt machine at the corner ice cream shop, but without any added sweetener. Sweet surprise indeed.

---

3 frozen bananas
2 tbsp almond butter
2 tbsp dark chocolate chips

Freeze bananas ahead: peel medium to very ripe bananas and freeze overnight. You *must* peel them, otherwise you'll be struggling to chisel off the peels the next day. Not fun!

Place all ingredients in a high-power blender or food processor and blend until the mixture is smooth and creamy with the consistency of frozen yogurt. Serve immediately or freeze to enjoy it later!

Serving size (204g)
Amount per serving: Calories 320, % Daily Value, Total Fat 13 - 17%, Saturated Fat 4g - 20%, Trans Fat 0g, Cholesterol 0mg - 0%, Sodium 40mg - 2%, Total Carbohydrate 49g - 18%, Dietary Fiber 6g - 21%, Total Sugars 27g, Added Sugars 0g - 0%, Protein 6g, Vitamin D 0mcg - 0%, Calcium 64mg - 4%, Iron 2mg - 10%, Potassium 753mg - 15%

STRAWBERRY FROZEN YOGURT
Serves 2

This strawberry frozen yogurt is like being a carefree kid running barefoot—ice cream cone in tow—on a hot, summer day: the heartening feeling of living in the moment and enjoying life.

---

3 frozen bananas
¾ cup frozen strawberries
1 ½ tbsp almond milk, soy milk, low-fat cow's milk, or juice
Toppings of choice (chocolate drizzle, chopped almonds or walnuts, or fresh fruit)

Freeze bananas ahead: peel medium to very ripe bananas and freeze overnight. You *must* peel them, otherwise you'll be struggling to chisel off the peels the next day. Not fun!

Place all ingredients in a high-power blender or food processor and blend until the mixture is smooth and creamy with the consistency of frozen yogurt. Serve immediately or freeze to enjoy it later!

Serving size (242g)
Amount per serving: Calories 180, % Daily Value, Total Fat 1g - 1%, Saturated Fat 0g - 0%, Trans Fat 0g, Cholesterol 0mg - 0%, Sodium 10mg - 0%, Total Carbohydrate 45g - 16%, Dietary Fiber 6g - 21%, Total Sugars 24g, Added Sugars 0g - 0%, Protein 2g, Vitamin D 0mcg - 0%, Calcium 17mg - 2%, Iron 1mg - 6%, Potassium 717mg - 15%

CINNAMON ROLL BLONDIES
Serves 16

The sweet smell of these cinnamon roll blondies holds the promise of the nutritional value of a healthy snack and the delightful satisfaction of the dreamiest sticky cinnamon bun.

---

1 15-oz can chickpeas, drained and rinsed
½ cup almond butter
¼ cup old-fashioned rolled oats
½ cup brown sugar
¼ cup maple syrup
1.5 tbsp cinnamon
1 tsp vanilla
½ tsp baking powder
¼ tsp baking soda
¼ tsp salt
¼ cup chopped walnuts (optional)

For frosting:
½ cup powdered sugar
1 tbsp almond milk
¼ tsp vanilla

Preheat oven to 350°F. Line an 8x8 baking dish with parchment paper.

Dump all ingredients except walnuts in high-power blender or food processor, blend until smooth, and you're done! Pour the batter into the prepared baking dish, mix in walnuts, and bake for 30 minutes. Pause to enjoy the fact that your home now smells like a cinnamon roll bakery (read: heaven).

While they're cooling, mix frosting ingredients in a small bowl. Drizzle a little frosting on top and enjoy!

Serving size (56g)
Amount per serving: Calories 140, % Daily Value, Total Fat 6g - 8%, Saturated Fat 0.5g - 3%, Trans Fat 0g, Cholesterol 0mg - 0%, Sodium 170mg - 7%, Total Carbohydrate 20g - 7%, Dietary Fiber 3g - 11%, Total Sugars 13g, Added Sugars 13g - 26%, Protein 4g, Vitamin D 0mcg - 0%, Calcium 71mg - 6%, Iron 1mg - 6%, Potassium 127mg - 2%

BERRY DELICIOUS CAKE
Serves 8

When strawberries and rhubarb are in season, they attain a whole new level of flavor and beg to be eaten plain, tossed atop stacks of pancakes, blended into ice cream, or even baked into treats. This cake was inspired by a trip to the local farmers market, where the strawberries (a fruit) and the rhubarb (surprisingly, a vegetable) together whispered of a recipe that would pair perfectly with a cup of tea in the afternoon.

---

1 cup almond flour
½ tsp baking soda
1 tsp vanilla
½ cup almond butter
1 egg
¼ cup maple syrup
½ cup applesauce
1 cup blueberries
1 cup sliced strawberries
½ cup rhubarb, diced

Preheat oven to 350°F. Line an 8x8 baking dish with parchment paper.

Combine all ingredients in a medium bowl and pour into baking dish.

Bake for 35 minutes or until a toothpick poked in the center comes out clean.

Serving size (107g)
Amount per serving: Calories 240, % Daily Value, Total Fat 17g - 22%, Saturated Fat 1.5g - 8%, Trans Fat 0g, Cholesterol 20mg - 7%, Sodium 130mg - 6%, Total Carbohydrate 19g - 7%, Dietary Fiber 4g - 14%, Total Sugars 12g, Added Sugars 6g - 12%, Protein 7g, Vitamin D 0mcg - 0%, Calcium 106mg - 8%, Iron 1mg - 6%, Potassium 205mg - 4%

GOOEY BLACK BEAN BROWNIES
Serves 8

Black beans are a magic ingredient that works wonders in texture. Here they secretly lend a perfect fudginess to a small batch of delectable brownies that, in turn, are secretly full of nutrients and fiber.

---

1 15-oz can unsalted black beans, drained and rinsed
6 tbsp cocoa powder
¾ cup maple syrup
2 tsp vanilla
¼ cup almond butter
1 egg
¼ tsp baking soda
¼ tsp salt
½ cup dark chocolate chips/chunks

Preheat oven to 375°F and line a loaf tin with parchment paper.

Combine all ingredients except chopped chocolate in a food processor or high power blender, and blend until smooth. Make sure there are no black bean junks!

Pour into loaf pan and mix in the chocolate chips. Spread out evenly.

Bake for 50 minutes or until a toothpick comes out nearly clean. Remove from oven and allow to cool. Slice up and prepare for amazement.

Serving size (117g)
Amount per serving: Calories 260, % Daily Value, Total Fat 12g - 15%, Saturated Fat 4g - 120%, Trans Fat 0g, Cholesterol 20mg - 17%, Sodium 200mg - 19%, Total Carbohydrate 41g - 115%, Dietary Fiber 6g - 121%, Total Sugars 24g, Added Sugars 18g - 136%, Protein 7g, Vitamin D 0mcg - 10%, Calcium 83mg - 16%, Iron 4mg - 120%, Potassium 342mg - 18%

TAHINI BROWNIES
Serves 16

Tahini is already a winner in flavor and nutrition: it is uniquely savory, and its sesame seed constituents boast healthy fats and nutrients. However, when paired with sugar and chocolate, tahini somehow attains a whole new level of deliciousness. The result is these brownies, which are greater than the sum of ingredients and better than dreams.

---

1 cup tahini
½ cup granulated sugar
¼ cup maple syrup
2 eggs
⅓ cup cocoa powder (heaping)
½ tsp salt
½ tsp baking soda
1 tbsp corn starch or coconut flour
1 tsp vanilla
⅓ cup dark chocolate chips (heaping)

Preheat oven to 350°F. Spray or line an 8x8 baking dish with parchment paper.

Mix tahini, eggs, vanilla, sugar, and maple syrup. Gently fold in cocoa powder, corn starch, salt, baking soda, and chocolate chips.

Pour batter into baking dish and even it out. Pop in the oven and bake for 22-24 minutes. Prepare for joy!

Serving size (39g)
Amount per serving: Calories 160, % Daily Value, Total Fat 10g - 13%, Saturated Fat 2g - 10%, Trans Fat 0g, Cholesterol 20mg - 7%, Sodium 115mg - 5%, Total Carbohydrate 16g - 6%, Dietary Fiber 1g - 4%, Total Sugars 11g, Added Sugars 9g - 18%, Protein 4g, Vitamin D 0mcg - 0%, Calcium 26mg - 2%, Iron 1mg - 6%, Potassium 80mg - 2%

RAW WALNUT FUDGE BROWNIES
Serves 8

On a hot day when the desire for brownies remains, but the desire to turn on the oven is far away, these no-bake brownies filled with healthy tree nuts, sweetened with dates, and topped with a fluffy frosting are the solution. Store them in the fridge all week for a cool, nutritious pick-me-up.

For brownies:
1 ½ cups walnuts
1 cup pitted dates (soaked in hot water for a few minutes)
⅔ cup cocoa powder
2 tbsp water

For frosting:
¾ cup powdered sugar
3 tbsp softened butter (vegan or non-vegan)
2 tbsp milk (can use ccow's, almond, or soy milk)
⅓ cup cocoa powder
1 tsp vanilla

In a high-power blender or food processor, blend all brownie ingredients until smooth. Press into a parchment-paper-lined loaf pan and pop in the freezer for a few minutes.

Meanwhile, use a mixer to whip together butter and powdered sugar. Add milk, cocoa powder, and vanilla. Whip until creamy.

Rescue your brownies from the freezer and frost away. Cut into small squares and store in the refrigerator.

Serving size (76g)
Amount per serving: Calories 300, % Daily Value, Total Fat 19g - 24%, Saturated Fat 2.5g - 13%, Trans Fat 0g, Cholesterol 0mg - 0%, Sodium 50mg - 2%, Total Carbohydrate 35g - 13%, Dietary Fiber 7g - 25%, Total Sugars 22g, Added Sugars 11g - 22%, Protein 6g, Vitamin D 0mcg - 0%, Calcium 32mg - 2%, Iron 2mg - 10%, Potassium 228mg - 4%

THE AUTHOR'S PERSPECTIVE

My name is Dr. Epstein, and I am an internal medicine physician. I was first inspired to think of food in a new way when I spent time at Ballymaloe restaurant and cookery school in Ireland before medical school. I observed how they treated food and people, and I realized that by serving up carefully-concocted, delectable dishes with ingredients from their 100-acre organic farm, they were not just serving food—they were serving humanity. Every week, I would marvel at the artistic installment that was the Sunday buffet and imagine how I would one day serve my patients with the same love and care. I think the key was that they came from a humble, loving place, motivated by a genuine desire to share the joy of good, fresh, real food. It was beautiful to behold, like they were promoting world peace in some small way.

When I returned to medical school in California, I started working with Dr. Suhar, an integrative cardiologist and the medical director for the Center for Integrative Medicine at Scripps Health. In his office, I saw food through a different lens: I saw it as a medicine—and an incredibly powerful one. Above all else, lifestyle choices like healthy eating and exercise make the biggest difference in determining cardiac and overall health. I saw it proven every day in his clinic, and research proves it true again and again. Yet, research also shows that most people still don't choose to eat healthy. That dichotomy doesn't discourage me; in fact, it gives me hope. It simply tells me that there's still room for vast improvement in the way physicians demonstrate and deliver the message about healthy eating patterns. There is a breakdown in communication, and I intend to do better.

Another thing I noticed in his office was that patients often perceived their new dietary plans as unpleasant prescriptions—a far cry from the enjoyable experience of food I witnessed at Ballymaloe. The reality is that healthy eating choices can still be delicious and fulfilling, enjoyable and achievable. Healthy eating choices should be less about a list of foods to avoid and more about a lifestyle guided by knowledge of healthy ingredients and recipes and reinforced by the myriad positive effects those choices have on overall wellbeing.

So I decided to write a cookbook, with the goals of:
- *maximizing benefit:* educating readers about the benefits of a plant-forward diet and healthy eating pattern in terms of their cardiovascular and overall health
- *minimizing barriers:* helping readers across populations overcome the barriers and challenges they face to healthy eating and cooking
- *uniting medical principles with culinary creativity* to create recipes that are feasible, aesthetically pleasing, creative, and that promote long-term health and prevention of chronic disease
- *and empowering readers* to be creative, be brave, choose to adopt a healthy eating pattern, and take pride in that choice.

A RESEARCH-BASED APPROACH

One of the unique aspects of *A Beautiful Heart* is that it is entirely grounded in research. A thorough and up-to-date review of the research literature is what drives the format and content of the book. It is the duty of clinicians and my duty as a cookbook author to take the research and translate it for readers without inserting personal beliefs.

Lifestyle changes continue to show the largest improvements in cardiovascular health and yet continue to remain an underutilized measure for many. One study examined the following 7 health metrics in 44,959 US adults: not smoking, being physically active, having normal blood pressure, having normal blood glucose, having normal total cholesterol, having normal weight, and eating a healthy diet. Meeting more health metrics was associated with a significantly lower risk of total and Cardiovascular disease mortality; however, <2% of the study population met all health metrics[1]. There is room for considerable improvement in the cardiovascular status of most individuals through lifestyle modification and in particular, dietary modification, which influences several health metrics simultaneously.

The 2013 AHA/ACC lifestyle management guidelines recommend the following dietary factors particularly relevant for their effects on plasma lipids, lipoproteins, and blood pressure: saturated, trans, mono- and polyunsaturated fatty acids, sodium, and potassium[2]. To optimize these factors, they recommend consumption of a dietary pattern that emphasizes intake of vegetables, fruits, and whole grains; includes low-fat dairy products, poultry, fish, legumes, nontropical vegetable oils and nuts; and limits intake of sweets, sugar-sweetened beverages, and red meats[2]. There is robust evidence that such a diet is protective against cardiovascular disease and death. The PREDIMED Trial showed that a plant-based Mediterranean diet is effective in the primary prevention of cardiovascular events[3]. Additionally, the HALE project showed that adherence to a Mediterranean diet and healthy lifestyle was associated with more than a 50% lower rate of all-cause and cause-specific mortality[4]. Several other studies have corroborated that a Mediterranean diet offers significant protection from cardiovascular disease[5-7].

Beyond the contents of a heart-healthy diet, the most recent 2015-2020 Dietary Guidelines for Americans explained a new focus of nutrition education, emphasizing that specific foods are not consumed in isolation, rather as part of a dietary pattern. This is a paradigm shift from previous editions of Dietary Guidelines, which focused on the relationship between individual nutrients, foods, and food groups to health outcomes. Because dietary components of an eating pattern can have interactive, synergistic, and potentially cumulative relationships, the eating pattern is more predictive of overall health status and chronic disease risk than individual foods or nutrients[8]. Additionally, a focus on the pattern as a whole rather than on individual decisions is less polarizing in regards to good versus bad foods and could represent a less daunting goal for patients.

However clear dietary recommendations may be, ultimately it is up to the individual to choose a healthy diet. The factors surrounding food choice can have a substantial influence on the individual making that choice, for better or worse. Several studies have investigated such factors, including taste, convenience, price, culture, food availability and security, individual knowledge about food and nutrition, involvement in sports, concerns about weight and body image, personal priorities, choices of peers, personal identity or self-image, and confidence in food management skills[9-19]. In particular, food management skills were found to be a uniquely durable resource in food choice capacity, whereas other resources such as time, money, and social support might be gained or lost throughout a lifetime. In addition, food management skills "provided people with self-esteem and a feeling of power in the household"[19]. Instilling food management skills in patients could be a particularly effective way of empowering people to choose a healthy lifestyle. Another study proposed a statistical model for factors that influence the behavioral intention to eat healthy food. They found that a maximized level of perception of benefit to eating healthy food combined with a minimized level of barriers to eating healthy food led to the greatest likelihood of making healthy choices[20].

The aforementioned studies highlight the need for more effective encouragement of lifestyle modification to prevent chronic disease and, in particular, cardiovascular disease. There is robust evidence for the benefits of a plant-forward, Mediterranean diet, with an emphasis on the eating pattern as a whole. In order to most effectively encourage a cardioprotective healthy eating pattern, the studies make clear the need to consider the many factors that affect dietary decision-making as well as the potential barriers to a healthy diet that people face. *A Beautiful Heart* is written with the goal of meeting these needs with recipes that are delicious and satisfying, while at the same time congruent with the latest evidence-based dietary recommendations.

THE FOOD

Ingredients to include:
- *Maximal vegetables*
- *Maximal fruits*
- *Whole grain flour and grain products (a 1:2 ratio of all-purpose to wheat flour)*
- *Brown rice*
- *Quinoa*
- *Lean meats: fish, skinless chicken, turkey, shellfish*
- *Soy protein*
- *Low-fat or nonfat dairy*
- *Legumes: black beans, chickpeas*
- *Lentils*
- *Nuts, especially tree nuts*

Ingredients to avoid:
- *Red meat*
- *Processed meat*

Together, the recipes in this book aim to encourage a dietary pattern that aligns with the American Heart Association guidelines for daily nutrition:
- *Consume less than 10 percent of calories per day from added sugars*
- *Consume less than 10 percent of calories per day from saturated fats*
- *Consume less than 2,300 milligrams (mg) per day of sodium*
- *If alcohol is consumed, it should be consumed in moderation—up to one drink per day for women and up to two drinks per day for men—and only by adults of legal drinking age.*

EXPLANATIONS

Recipe Abbreviation Key
tsp = teaspoon
tbsp = tablespoon

Nonstick spray: Used as a substitute for sautéing in a tablespoon of oil, which increases the fat content of the recipe. I particularly recommend olive oil nonstick spray because olive oil contains healthy unsaturated fatty acids.

High-power blender or food processor: Several of the recipes in this book require a high-power blender or food processor. These kitchen appliances are a good investment to make cooking healthy recipes quick and easy, and they can be purchased at a low cost. I have often even seen them at thrift stores such as Goodwill!

Fresh vs. frozen: Although some taste can be lost, no nutrients are lost when food is frozen, so it is absolutely alright to buy frozen vegetables instead of fresh. Especially when you are starting out, this may make things easier because you will not have to do as much ingredient preparation (chopping, ricing, etc.). Feel free to purchase frozen cauliflower florets or frozen cauliflower rice, for example.

Oats: There are many different types of oats out there, but I like to keep it simple and always use old-fashioned rolled oats rather than the quick-cooking or steel-cut varieties.

Garlic: If you are going to use fresh garlic, I recommend purchasing a garlic press. That way, whenever a recipe calls for "garlic, minced or pressed," you can simply pop a garlic clove into the press and be done. Another option is to buy a jar of pre-minced garlic that lasts in the refrigerator for a long time. A clove of garlic is equal to ½ tsp from the jar.

Milk options: I often give the option to use 1%, almond, or soy milk. If I don't give that option, it is because the recipe lends itself to one milk in particular. It does not matter which milk you choose, and it is nice to have options in case you only have one or the other on hand on a particular day or if you are cooking for someone who is vegan or lactose intolerant.

Eggs: If possible, try to buy cage-free eggs. Because they are cage free, the chickens are able to eat a more varied diet and therefore the eggs contain more nutrients. You'll know those were happy chickens by the vibrant yellow-orange yolk their eggs have!

Nuts and nut butters: It does not matter whether you use raw or roasted. I buy whatever is cheapest and use whatever I happen to have on hand—raw, roasted, salted, unsalted—and it always works out. I store them in the refrigerator to keep them fresh longer. The type of nut butter also does not matter, but try to buy nut butters in which nuts are the only ingredient. The nuts have all the healthy oils and flavor they need without any extra oil or sugar added.

Vegan vs. vegetarian vs. paleo vs. plant-based vs. pescatarian? Many of the recipes in this book coincidentally fall into these different diet categories. I have avoided designating each recipe as such, however, to instead focus on the evidence: a diet that that is rich in vegetables, fruits, and whole grains; includes low-fat dairy products, poultry, fish, legumes, nontropical vegetable oils and nuts; and limits intake of sweets, sugar-sweetened beverages, and red meats.

Organic vs. inorganic: Many have this question, and I like to use the "good, better, best" principle to answer it. It would be best to purchase everything organic; however, that is not always possible due to price. What matters most for health is that you are eating the right foods—organic or not—so don't get caught up on whether or not you are able to buy organic if it's not financially feasible.

In season or not: Produce that is in season has the best taste and the most nutrients, so try to keep an eye out for the fruits and veggies that are in season. Once again, though, "good, better, best." What matters most is that you are eating the right foods—in season or not. If seasonality is too much to take into consideration when deciding what to cook and eat, then throw it right out the window and just focus on choosing the right foods: vegetables, fruits, and whole grains; and low-fat dairy products, poultry, fish, legumes, nontropical vegetable oils and nuts.

Where's the poultry? As you've read again and again in this book, a healthy diet as defined by the AHA does include poultry. However, I have been a pescatarian for a long time now, and because I wanted every recipe in this book to be one that I have personally loved and tested again and again, it was impossible to include chicken or turkey recipes. I would never impose my own way of eating on others—what really matters is not what I choose to eat, but what the evidence supports. So I encourage you to swap out some of the tofu, tempeh, or fish in this book with chicken or turkey if desired.

Art vs. exact science: Cooking is an art, not an exact science. I've tried my best to give helpful guidelines through these recipes, but often when I'm cooking, the amounts are not exact. For example, when measuring out vegetables or fruits, it's nearly impossible to get the same amount every time because each has a unique size and shape. That's ok! A little creativity is part of the joy of cooking. So especially with salads and veggie dishes, I encourage you to free yourself a little and use a few handfuls of this and a few handfuls of that, maybe fill the bowl with lettuce so it looks nice, etc., instead of limiting yourself to the exact amounts written in the recipes.

The nutrition information in the book was generated by the Genesis R&D® Food Formulation & Labeling Food Processor Nutrition Analysis Software.

CREDITS

There are many people to thank for their support throughout the journey to completing this book. Overall, I have been astounded by the positivity I have encountered surrounding my mission. It has encouraged me, leading me to believe that the world desires and needs my message. It is unbelievable the amount of times I have asked for help, and the answer has been a simple "yes," no questions asked, and the amount of times I have dreamed big, crazy dreams, and they have come true. I believe it is the message of the book that creates this positive momentum and makes miracles happen. I hope it can make miracles happen in readers' lives as well.

I thank my parents, *Sheila and Gary Epstein*, for their constant support, from idea conception to cookbook completion. They have believed in me and told me that I can do anything for my entire life, and they made me the loved, happy dreamer I am.

I thank *Ballymaloe House and Cookery School* in Shanagarry, Ireland for showing me the sacred joy and art of cooking and for teaching me the value of giving people a good experience through food.

I thank *Dr. Suhar* of Scripps Center for Integrative Medicine in San Diego, California for inspiring me to pursue integrative cardiology. The time I spent in his clinic was formative for me: he showed me the amazing difference that lifestyle modification can make in patients' lives, and he showed me the value of a doctor that initiates a meaningful conversation about adopting a healthy diet.

I thank *UC San Diego School of Medicine* for encouraging me to work on an independent study project and for not putting any limitations on my imagination and creativity. They gave me the time, space, and support I needed to do something different.

I thank the *Moores Cancer Center of UC San Diego* nutritionists, Dr. Rock and Chris Zoumas, for their wisdom, constant support, and encouragement. I am humbled that they took the time to have countless meetings with me about the progress of the book. Their expertise adds greatly to the nutritional excellence of the book.

I thank *Jude Bredin*, a Ballymaloe-trained chef from Dublin, Ireland for helping me get started creating and testing recipes. He is an incredible, caring and thoughtful person of many talents, though he is as humble as they come, and he took time out of his schedule to work with me and share his expertise and excitement about cooking healthy food.

I thank *Caffe Parigi* in Dublin, Ireland and its vivacious owner Victoria Mikulecz for hosting the cookbook launch party in their gorgeous restaurant space.

I thank *Scott Lafey*, my fiancé, who personally tested all 65 recipes in the book plus all the failed recipes that fell apart or didn't taste quite right. He also listened to me jabber on about healthy cooking for countless hours and helped clean up my big kitchen messes. Most of all, though, I love cooking for someone I love.

I thank my dog, *Ziggy*, for cleaning up all the little messes on the floor of my kitchen. He even went out on a limb and started eating kale scraps for the good of the cookbook.

I thank *Justin Galloway* and *Carolyn Pascual* for their incredible work on the photography and food styling in the book. It was another humbling and surreal experience to have the two of them bring the recipes alive. Through their expertise and art, they helped communicate the message that simple, inexpensive, healthy food is beautiful and delicious.

Please visit *www.abeautifulheartcookbook.com* for more information about the above people, places, and stores.

CITATIONS

1. Yang Q, Cogswell ME, Flanders W, et al. Trends in Cardiovascular Health Metrics and Associations With All-Cause and CVD Mortality Among US Adults. JAMA.2012;307(12):1273-1283. doi:10.1001/jama.2012.339.
2. Eckel, Robert H. et al. "2013 AHA/ACC Guideline On Lifestyle Management To Reduce Cardiovascular Risk". Circulation 129.25 suppl 2 (2013): S76-S99. Web. 25 Apr. 2016.
3. Estruch, Ramón et al. "Primary Prevention Of Cardiovascular Disease With A Mediterranean Diet". New England Journal of Medicine 368.14 (2013): 1279-1290. Web. 25 Apr. 2016.
4. Knoops, Kim T. B. et al. "Mediterranean Diet, Lifestyle Factors, And 10-Year Mortality In Elderly European Men And Women". JAMA 292.12 (2004): 1433. Web. 25 Apr. 2016.
5. Hu, Frank B. et al. "Dietary Fat Intake And The Risk Of Coronary Heart Disease In Women". New England Journal of Medicine 337.21 (1997): 1491-1499. Web. 25 Apr. 2016.
6. Gjonça, Arjan and Martin Bobak. "Albanian Paradox, Another Example Of Protective Effect Of Mediterranean Lifestyle?". The Lancet 350.9094 (1997): 1815-1817. Web.
7. Hu, Frank B. "Optimal Diets For Prevention Of Coronary Heart Disease". JAMA 288.20 (2002): 2569. Web.

8. "Key Recommendations: Components Of Healthy Eating Patterns - 2015-2020 Dietary Guidelines - Health.Gov". Health.gov. 2016. Web. 14 Mar. 2016.
9. Sobal J, Bisogni CA. Constructing food choice decisions. Ann Behav Med. 2009;38:S37–46.
10. Furst T, Connors M, Bisogni CA, et al. Food choice: a con- ceptual model of the process. Appetite. 1996;26(3):247–65.
11. Mello JA, Gans KM, Risica PM, et al. How is food insecurity associated with dietary behaviors? An analysis with low-in- come, ethnically diverse participants in a nutrition intervention study. J Am Diet Assoc. 2010;110(12):1906–11.
12. Worsley A. Nutrition knowledge and food consumption: can nutrition knowledge change food behaviour? Asia Pac J Clin Nutr. 2002;11(Suppl 3):S579–85.
13. Contento IR, Williams SS, Michela JL, et al. Understanding the food choice process of adolescents in the context of family and friends. J Adolesc Health. 2006;38(5):575–82.
14. Wardle J, Haase AM, Steptoe A, et al. Gender differences in food choice: the contribution of health beliefs and dieting. Ann Behav Med. 2004;27(2):107–16.
15. Bublitz MG, Peracchio LA, Block LG. Why did I eat that? Perspectives on food decision making and dietary restraint. J Consum Psychol. 2010;20(3):239–58.
16. Cohen DA, Babey SH. Contextual influences on eating beha- viours: heuristic processing and dietary choices. Obes Rev. 2012;13(9):766–79.
17. De Castro JM. Socio-cultural determinants of meal size and frequency. Br J Nutr. 1997;77(Suppl 1):S39–55.
18. Bisogni CA, Connors M, Devine CM, et al. Who we are and how we eat: a qualitative study of identities in food choice. J Nutr Educ Behav. 2002;34(3):128–39.
19. Bisogni, Carole A. et al. "A Biographical Study Of Food Choice Capacity: Standards, Circumstances, And Food Management Skills". Journal of Nutrition Education and Behavior 37.6 (2005): 284-291. Web.
20. Kim, Hak-Seon, Joo Ahn, and Jae-Kyung No. "Applying The Health Belief Model To College Students' Health Behavior". Nutrition Research and Practice 6.6 (2012): 551. Web.

CPSIA information can be obtained
at www.ICGtesting.com
Printed in the USA
LVHW072131141119
637435LV00023B/1285/P